Endorsements

Consider this a sequel to The Lean Startup. The "10% Wins" strategy will take your MVP to the next level. A must-read!
—Nathan Chan, publisher of *Foundr Magazine*

Cadence is everything a business book should be: short, sharp and shareable.
—Jon Acuff, author of *Finish, Do Over and Start.*

Cadence is the perfect guide for any entrepreneur who wants to grow their company to the next level—fast. Pete Williams' 7 Levers framework is an ingenious tool that will bring immediate, repeatable results to your business. Read this book this morning and implement the lessons this afternoon.
—Mike Michalowicz, author of *Profit First*

Cadence is a must-read for any entrepreneur or business owner who wants to consistently and continually grow their business. It gives you more than growth "hacks" for small growth or wins—it gives you a complete framework that lets you leverage those small wins into major returns on your business.
—Robert Allen, author of *One Minute Millionaire* and *Multiple Streams of Income*

Cadence is an excellent book I highly recommend for anyone in the world of entrepreneurship. Not only is it a compelling story that will hit close to home for entrepreneurs facing similar challenges, Williams also made sure readers would walk away with practical advice that can be applied in any business.

—Clate Mask, CEO and co-founder of Infusionsoft

I usually dread business books, but the power of this story hooked me and I found myself addicted. It's such a fun and captivating story that the lessons of the book found their way into my daily business behaviors without my even trying.

—Doug O'Brien, author of *Step Up to Mastery*
and *The User's Guide to Sleight of Mouth*

The impact of 10% Wins and the power of the 7 Levers framework is something that every business owner or growth hacker must embrace. It will make such a profound impact on your bottom line.

—David Jenyns, author of *Authority Content*

I checked out my family tree a few years ago to see it was full of employees. Not a small-business owner in sight. No wonder I have such respect for them. Starting one takes guts. Making one profitable takes guts, brains and a little luck. To minimize the luck factor, read Cadence. Now. Go.

—Tim Reid, host of *The Small Business Big Marketing Show*

Whether you're an entrepreneur whose business currently earns seven figures or a startup founder who has yet to start building your vision, you need to read this book. The strategies Pete shares will reframe your thinking and focus you on the areas most critical for growing your business.

—Dr. Nicole Lipkin, author of What Keeps Leaders Up at Night

Cadence has the kind of magnetic flow that keeps you turning the pages. It's an engaging 'must-read' for any entrepreneur or student wanting to learn what it takes to drive a business to new levels of profitability.

—Alfred Deakin Professor Mike Ewing, Executive Dean, Faculty of Business & Law. Deakin University

The 7 levers are simple, but powerful. They have the ability to transform your business.

—Scott Pape, The Barefoot Investor

GOLD MEDAL WINNER: 2018 NON-FICTION BOOK AWARDS
SILVER MEDAL WINNER: 2018 AXIOM BUSINESS BOOK AWARDS
BRONZE MEDAL WINNER: 2018 AMERICAN BUSINESS AWARDS (STEVIE)
WINNER [BUSINESS]: 2018 INDEPENDENT PRESS AWARD
WINNER [BUSINESS]: 2018 LOS ANGELES BOOK FESTIVAL
FINALIST [BUSINESS]: 2018 INTERNATIONAL BOOK AWARDS

CADENCE

CADENCE

A TALE OF FAST BUSINESS GROWTH

WITHDRAWN

PETE WILLIAMS

NEW YORK

LONDON • NASHVILLE • MELBOURNE • VANCOUVER

CADENCE
A TALE OF FAST BUSINESS GROWTH

Published in New York, New York, by Morgan James Publishing. Morgan James is a trademark of Morgan James, LLC. www.MorganJamesPublishing.com

The Morgan James Speakers Group can bring authors to your live event. For more information or to book an event visit The Morgan James Speakers Group at www.TheMorganJamesSpeakersGroup.com.

ISBN 9781600379703 paperback
ISBN 9781600379710 eBook
Library of Congress Control Number: 2017916969

Cover Design by:
Rachel Lopez
www.r2cdesign.com

Interior Design by:
Chris Treccani
www.3dogcreative.net

Interior Graphics by:
Nathan Fisher
www.NathanFisher.com

In an effort to support local communities, raise awareness and funds, Morgan James Publishing donates a percentage of all book sales for the life of each book to Habitat for Humanity Peninsula and Greater Williamsburg.

Get involved today! Visit
www.MorganJamesBuilds.com

Dedication

For all the entrepreneurs and small business owners who lie awake at night, changing the world.

Table of Contents

"Profit is what happens when you do everything else right."
—Yvon Chouinard (Founder of Patagonia)

Preface

This is a story about how to consistently grow your business, and how small improvements in just seven key areas will double your profits—fast.

It's the tale of a business owner and triathlon coach named JJ who left his stable job as a teacher to fulfill his dream of becoming an entrepreneur. Unfortunately, two years after opening his bike shop, Cadence, JJ finds himself in a place that is all too familiar to most business owners—struggling to stay afloat, unsure of what to do next, and lacking a strategic plan to grow profits.

His luck turns around once he meets Charlie, a budding first-time IRONMAN who has hired JJ as his training coach. JJ soon realizes that there is more to Charlie than meets the eye. An experienced and successful businessman, Charlie soon becomes a coach and mentor to JJ as well.

Over the course of twenty weeks, as JJ helps Charlie get ready for the grueling IRONMAN triathlon, Charlie shares his secrets with JJ and helps him drastically change the trajectory and profits of Cadence by using a strategy he calls "*10% Wins*."

While this story is fictional, JJ's experiences are very real for many people who own and operate their own businesses—offline or online, retail or wholesale, product or service. Every day across the globe, more than 27 million small business owners open their doors and feel instant overwhelm and confusion. They experience this silent panic because most of them have absolutely no idea what they need to do each day to grow their business profits. Usually, they try to solve this problem by working longer hours, investing in courses to improve their skills, iterating their product over and over, or chasing the latest marketing trend. Some may even just stick their heads in the sand because the thought of dealing with the problem is too overwhelming and they don't know where to begin.

But action and achievement are not the same thing. Working longer or harder will only help you succeed if you have a strategy behind what you do. Otherwise, all of that effort could easily add up to nothing.

This book provides a framework embraced around the world as the *"7 Levers"* and an action plan you can cycle through to exponentially grow your profits by achieving small, key wins in these seven areas—these are the *10% Wins*.

Loosely inspired by a true story, JJ and Charlie's journey is based on an amalgam of the more than fifteen years I have spent in business—as an employee, marketing strategist, and an owner of multiple businesses—online and offline, B2B and B2C, and in everything from e-commerce to catering.

Throughout my journey, I've made more mistakes and lost more money than I care to admit, yet I have been lucky enough to have great business partners and mentors who've collectively added to all my successes. These people, and the lessons I've learned, inspired the character of Charlie.

Whatever is motivating you to create a more rewarding business, I hope you find the tale of JJ and Charlie a catalyst for your own series of *10% Wins* and a more profitable business cadence of your own!

Pete Williams
#CadenceBook

Chapter 1

Falling Behind

"Always good to see you, Ted," JJ said as he rang up the last sale of the day—a pair of cycling gloves—and bagged the item for his customer who had almost, *almost*, gone home with a new set of $3,000 race wheels instead.

JJ smiled as he bid farewell to Ted, but the smile faded the minute he stepped out the door. One of the store's regulars, Ted always wanted to stay for a long chat whenever he came in. His visits were always pleasant, but they rarely paid off in terms of sales. But how could JJ say, "No, I can't talk," to someone who helped keep the lights on in the place? With the sound of the register still jingling in his ears, JJ locked the door, turned over the "closed" sign, and moved back to his stool behind the checkout counter.

He opened his laptop and looked at the numbers again. They couldn't be right. He was sure his sales had been on an upswing this quarter, but the figure—in red—told a different story.

Feeling an all-too-familiar knot in his stomach, JJ shut down the computer and grabbed his training bag. Dammit, he was running late again. If he left right now, he could be at the track just before his training squad arrived at six o'clock for their first coaching session of the season.

As JJ locked up the store, he felt a cool breeze coming off the beach nearby. Walking through the parking lot to his Jeep, he took a moment to inhale the salty sea air and watch the seagulls flying overhead. The fresh air provided a temporary relief from the stress of the day, but as he climbed into his Jeep, JJ reflected on just how he had arrived at this point. Two years ago he had quit his stable-but-far-from-lucrative job as a high-school gym teacher to try his hand at entrepreneurship. He'd opened Cadence Bike Shop in the hopes he could marry his passion for cycling—especially triathlons—with the lifelong desire he'd had to run his own business.

Nobody knew more about bikes and triathlon racing than JJ. He had completed the Hawaii IRONMAN World Championships an amazing five times. His triathlon training squad had grown through word-of-mouth to include as many as thirty-seven athletes per season—some of whom he'd been training for years—and he'd become one of the most popular and respected coaches in the area.

JJ hadn't always been an athlete. For much of his childhood, he was overweight and out of shape, always falling behind his classmates in gym and consistently being picked last for team sports. He'd suffered a fair amount of taunts because of his weight, the cruelest of which was a play on his name. "Hey there, PB&JJ!" the other kids would shout.

That all changed his first year of high school. After spending his summer vacation largely indoors, JJ stepped on the scale at the beginning of his first gym class of the year and was shocked to find he'd gained twenty pounds in just a few months. In that moment, something in JJ's mind clicked and he knew he had to start doing things differently.

When the coach sent him and the other students outside to run laps, JJ stood at the head of the track, shuffling his feet from side to side and staring at the black tarmac that stretched out before him. It looked long, intimidatingly long. *I can do this*, a voice inside him said. It seemed to come from out of nowhere, but it was undeniably his voice. *I can do this*, the voice repeated. Somehow, the newly sparked fire within him had fueled a determination to change, to leave PB&JJ far behind. And he ran…

He'd been an athlete ever since and ended up joining both the track and swim teams in high school. In college, he discovered cycling, and triathlons quickly became his passion. He loved the solitude of the sport—especially the training—and the feeling that your number one competitor was always yourself. He'd become a teacher so he could help kids find their confidence and get healthy through physical activity, just like he had done. Sometimes, especially on days like today, he missed it and almost forgot why he left.

Thinking back on his younger days, JJ flexed his forearms as he gripped the wheel of the Jeep, proud of the way his muscles rippled as he tensed them. But the reverie was quickly interrupted as his thoughts turned back to his business. When he'd been a teenager, he'd worked his butt off to get in shape, and, even though it took time, the effort had paid off. Now he was working just as hard, and for what? Lately it seemed like triathlon coaching—a side gig he'd started to generate extra income while teaching—was more profitable than the sales from his bike shop.

Cadence had started out promising. As one of the only specialty cycling stores in town, local athletes had flocked to the place when it first opened, eager to get JJ's expert advice on the latest gear. But now—two years later—he'd seen little-to-no growth, and the store was barely breaking even. He'd hoped Cadence would allow him to generate more income than he'd made as a teacher or coach—that over time, he'd be able to make more money with less effort and finally take some time away to spend with his family. But lately it hardly seemed worth it. He was working more than ever, and the strain was starting to show. Not only was he falling behind on his accounts with a few key suppliers, but he could see the toll the situation was taking on his wife, Sarah, and their three-year-old twins, Ben and Emily.

Sarah had taken time off from her job as an accountant to stay home with the twins until they started school, but had been forced to go back to work part-time to compensate for the salary JJ had had to defer for the past few quarters. She never complained, and she enjoyed working, but JJ could read the concern on her face, and it broke his heart. Starting his own business was supposed to allow him to provide a better life for his family, and here he was making things worse.

JJ forced himself to stop thinking about the store as he pulled into the track. *Things will get better*, he told himself. *They have to.*

* * * * *

A former horse-training track that encircled a botanical garden, the 2.4-mile loop was a magnet for the city's athletes and weekend warriors alike. Towering trees kept it shady and scenic, and one side of the loop meandered along the city riverfront, with the downtown skyscrapers forming a backdrop.

JJ felt his adrenaline surge as he parked the Jeep and changed into his running shoes. A guy could lose himself in the rhythmic *crunch-crunch-crunch-crunch* of his feet against the soft gravel track, leaving the stresses of business ownership far behind for a couple of hours. He knew he'd have to address the issue at some point—tighten his belt, figure something out—but for now, he just couldn't wait to get out there and run.

He checked his phone to remind himself of tonight's newcomers. The first session of the season always meant some new and eager faces. He saw three new people on the lineup: two who, according to their registration forms, wanted to lose a few pounds and train for their first competitive event—a short sprint-distance triathlon—and one who was training for the grueling IRONMAN distance—a 2.4-mile (3.86 km) swim, a 112-mile (180.25 km) ride, and a marathon 26.2-mile (42.2 km) run.

The track was packed as it always was on a warm spring evening like this particular Tuesday night. "JJ, I haven't forgotten about you…I'll try and get in this weekend to buy the new helmet and aero-bars," a voice called.

JJ didn't even have time to turn around before Scott Wilson, a fellow triathlete he knew from the local competitive circuit, flew past him at what seemed like an Olympic sprint pace. Scott had been telling JJ that for months. It seemed like he had more supposed sales coming in this week than he'd had actual sales in the past month.

Scott was a good guy, but hearing, "I'll buy it soon," actually made JJ feel worse. His bank manager wasn't buying that line from him any longer—and neither was Sarah.

"How's it going, JJ?" one of his regulars said as he made his way to the usual meet-up spot where a few of the early birds were already doing their warm-up stretches.

"Evening, Tracy," JJ said. "Did everybody have a nice off-season? Looks like you guys are itchin' to run again." This time his smile was genuine as he fist-bumped his athletes while the rest of the squad filtered in. In all, twenty-odd people turned up and stood in a loose cluster while JJ addressed them.

"Welcome everyone!" JJ could feel some of the tension of the day release as he eased into his coaching mode. Training motivated athletes like the ones standing in front of him always energized JJ, even if just for a few hours. "I'm glad to see some of you have come back for more. For those of you who are new, we're glad to have you!"

JJ noted the three newcomers among the familiar faces in the crowd. He took note of a tall dark-haired young man, probably in his early 30s, who clearly had the body of an athlete. *This must be my IRONMAN rookie*, he thought as he stepped over to introduce himself.

"You must be Charlie," JJ said, extending his hand. "Glad to have you on the squad." JJ had a habit of Googling each of his trainees before meeting them, mostly to see if he could get a sense of their level of fitness. Charlie, he'd noticed, had competed in a few local events where he'd posted some decent times. He'd also learned that Charlie was a successful local businessman, having founded two companies and invested in many others. *Maybe*, JJ had thought at the time, *I can pick his brain a bit during our one-on-one sessions*. It depressed JJ to know just how desperate he'd become.

"Glad to be here," Charlie said, an infectious grin spreading across his face. "Your reputation precedes you, so don't go easy on me."

"That's one thing I never do," JJ said, laughing. "By the time I'm finished with you, you'll be world-class."

After introducing himself to the other new athletes, JJ sent the regulars off on a ten-minute warm-up run around the track. To motivate and outline the plan for the training, he shared one of his favorite stories with the newbies.

"Welcome to the squad," he began. "Before we get into your formal training, I want to tell you a story that pretty much captures my approach to coaching." He cleared his throat before continuing. "In 2010, British cycling coach Dave Brailsford faced a tough task. No British cyclist had ever won the Tour de France, cycling's toughest event. But as the new general manager and performance director for Team Sky, Great Britain's pro team, that's exactly what Brailsford set out to do.

"His approach was simple. Brailsford believed in a concept that's referred to as the "aggregation of marginal gains." 1% margin for improvement in everything you do is how he explains it.

"Brailsford believed that if the team improved every area related to cycling by just *1%*, those tiny gains would add up to a remarkable improvement—and maybe even a Tour victory. The team started by optimizing the things you'd probably expect: rider nutrition, their training program, the ergonomics of the bike seat, and the weight of the tires." He saw Charlie nodding, his eyes shining. *Maybe he's heard this story before,* JJ thought.

"But Brailsford didn't stop there. He searched for 1% improvements in obscure areas that were overlooked by almost every other team. He figured out which pillow offered the best sleep and packed one for each team member when they traveled. He tested for the most effective type of massage gel, and taught riders the best way to wash their hands to avoid infection. Brailsford was convinced that if they could successfully execute as many 1% improvements as possible, then Team Sky would be in a position to maybe win the Tour de France in five years' time."

JJ paused here for dramatic effect. "He was wrong," he continued. "They won it in three years."

JJ always told this story to new team members because he wanted to emphasize how the combination of small, incremental gains could compound over time and why results didn't simply depend on how fast you could run, bike, or swim. Everything you did to prepare yourself for race day—from how much sleep you got, to your diet and your stress level—affected performance.

"It's not just about 'miles in the legs,'" he summarized as the trainees continued their warm-up stretches. "Sometimes in life, effort does not equate to outcome."

No sooner were the words out of his mouth than JJ thought about his long hours in the bike shop. *How ironic.*

After sending the other rookies off to join the rest of the group for a run around the track, JJ motioned for Charlie to stay put a moment.

"So, Charlie, you're training for your first IRONMAN, right?"

"That's right, coach," Charlie grinned. Something about the young man intrigued JJ. He carried himself with an easy confidence that suggested there was more to him than met the eye.

"That's great," JJ said. "We're going to have a lot of fun. According to your sign-up form, you're registered for the race in New Zealand about five months from now, yeah? So you've decided to travel to compete?"

"Yeah, I figured since I was going to be spending so much time away from my wife as I trained over the next few months, I might as well use it as an excuse to take her on a great vacation at the end of it. She deserves it, after all."

So does Sarah, JJ thought, wishing he could spare some time away from the store to spend more quality time with his wife.

"Right, well, that gives us twenty weeks to get you ready," JJ said, shifting his focus back to Charlie. "Why don't you come by my shop on Thursday evening so we can discuss your goals and work out a customized training plan to complement the group sessions?"

"Cadence Bike Shop on Third Avenue, right?" Charlie said. "The one out by the beach?"

JJ was impressed. Clearly Charlie had done his homework, too. "That's the one. Say, five-thirty? That way I can still make it home for a late supper without upsetting my wife too much."

"I'll be there," Charlie said, reaching to shake JJ's hand before loping off around the track.

Chapter 2

The Pressure Builds

The early Thursday morning swim session with the squad had run a little overtime, and now JJ was late to open the store. As he searched through his sports bag for the shop keys, he could hear the phone ringing inside.

That may be a customer, he thought as he fumbled with the lock and finally pushed the door open. Once inside, he tossed his bag behind the counter and reached for the phone, but it stopped ringing before he could pick up. After a few seconds, he noticed the red light indicating he had a voicemail.

"Hi JJ. It's Julia from ProSport Supplies calling. I'm just checking in to see how business is at Bayside's best bike shop. If you're not answering your phone, you must be with a customer. Hope you're

11

selling him one of our bikes! I'll try to call again a little later. Hope you're well. Bye."

As soon as he heard Jules's voice, JJ was relieved he hadn't answered the call. ProSport was one of his largest suppliers—and the one to whom he currently owed the most money. He'd already asked to defer his regular sixty-day payment by an extra thirty days, but he still had no idea how he was going to make it. He'd known Jules for years—since they both competed in the local triathlon circuit—but today was not the day to ask her for more time.

Half an hour later, he was joined by Dale, the youngest of his sales associates, and Matt, the store mechanic and de-facto manager when JJ wasn't around. "How's it going boss?" Dale called as he removed his bike helmet and headed to the break room to stash his stuff. All of JJ's employees were athletes. Matt and Jess, another sales associate in her early 30s, were road cyclists, and Emma, the other salesperson, was a runner. But Dale was in a class by himself.

At just twenty-two years old, Dale was a semi-pro triathlete and was making a real name for himself on the local race circuit. He had worked at the store since it had opened, and having him on staff had proven useful in getting other area athletes, many of whom were Dale's friends, into the store since they trusted Dale's expertise on what gear was best. Unfortunately, Dale wasn't all that effective at turning these potential customers into actual customers and often ended up spending more time talking about triathlons than he did selling equipment to triathletes. It had occurred to JJ on more than one occasion that Dale probably considered his job at Cadence an afterthought next to his training regimen, but he figured having someone like Dale on staff lent the store some extra credibility among the more serious athletes in town.

"Hanging in there, Dale," JJ said. There was no need to burden his staff with his financial problems at the moment. *It's just a seasonal slump,* JJ told himself. *Things will pick up soon—the season is just starting.*

The hours passed quickly, even though business was disappointingly slow. Fifteen minutes to closing time, Charlie walked in the door for the planning session he'd scheduled with JJ the week before. JJ motioned to meet him, but the store phone rang again so he double-backed and gestured to Charlie that he'd only be a second. Charlie gave him a knowing wink and walked over to a wall full of shiny new time-trial road bikes.

"Hey, slow poke," the voice said as JJ picked up the receiver.

It was Jules again. She was always ribbing JJ about his race times, but today he thought she might be referring to his payment terms instead.

"Hey you," JJ replied, trying not to sound nervous. "What's going on?"

"Lots of good stuff as always," Jules said. "Summer's coming, so things are getting busy here at the office. I trust they are for you, too?" Luckily she continued before JJ was forced to respond. "So did you get them?"

"Get what?" JJ asked, confused.

"The customer this morning! I assumed you were busy selling a new customer one of our fine steeds when I rang earlier, which is why you didn't pick up the phone." Jules often referred to ProSport bikes by names like "steed" or "chariot"—anything but "bike." It usually amused JJ, but not today.

"Oh yeah, yeah," JJ replied, not wanting to tell Jules that he had actually been doing his best Mary Poppins impression, trying to find the store keys at the bottom of his bag, when she had called that morning.

As he and Jules traded some small talk, JJ watched Dale approach Charlie, clearly not knowing who he was or why he was there. Dale carried himself like the athlete he was and always seemed to wear the staff uniform—a Cadence-branded cycling jersey—one size too small so he could show off his toned core.

"Need any help?" Dale asked, as lazily and disinterested as he usually was this close to the end of his shift. The longer he stuck around helping customers, the less time he'd have to work out that night.

JJ winced at the indifference oozing off Dale, knowing that a successful businessman like Charlie could probably sense it a mile away.

"No, I'm just looking around," Charlie said, releasing Dale of his duties.

"Cool, man. Well, the sale bikes are on the far wall over there. There are some great bargains to be had. Just let me know if you have any questions." This was Dale's typical clichéd approach to sales and customer service—reactive instead of proactive.

As Charlie continued to look around the store, JJ wrapped up his conversation with Jules.

"Hey, I'm going to be in Bayside next month. Can I book a time to catch up with you? Say 2 p.m. on Thursday the 11th?"

"Yeah, sure," JJ said, still annoyed at Dale's lame interaction with Charlie. "The 11th is fine." JJ wondered if Jules knew he was uneasy about their phone call.

"Fantastic, I'll put it on the calendar. And speaking of calendar, can I pencil in a date to tell Dave when to expect a payment on your account?"

There it was.

JJ's lips tightened into a straight line. "I can make it by the end of the month. I already talked to Dave about extending my terms this time around."

JJ wasn't confident he'd be able to make this payment, but if all else failed, he could put it on the company card. Using a credit card to pay key accounts was a trick JJ's accountant had taught him when he first opened the store. Not only did it help his cashflow by using the interest-free period as a way to extend his credit terms that little bit more, but the reward points he accumulated each year were enough to take his family on a small vacation. It certainly wasn't the dream life JJ had envisioned when he'd become an entrepreneur, but it was better than nothing, and certainly more than he could afford on the profits—or lack thereof—from the store.

"Thanks, JJ. You're the best. By the way, do you know why Dave and the rest of the accounts team don't ride?"

"No. Why?"

"Because they tend to lose their balance!" Jules laughed at her own joke as she hung up the phone. JJ chuckled despite himself.

JJ hung up the phone and called over to Charlie, who was still perusing the store. "Hey, champ, I'm just shutting the register off. I'll be with you in a second."

"Nice shop you got here," Charlie said, admiring a wall of high-end race wheels designed for the serious competitor, complemented by a range of mid-priced bicycles for recreational cyclists along the adjacent wall. There was even a row of kids' bikes. Cycling accessories, clothing, shoes, and helmets rounded out the store's fare. A large flat-screen TV on the back wall ran a slick video loop of high-performance equipment and old race footage—courtesy of a manufacturer, of course.

The shop was small but impressive; JJ knew it. Only one thing was missing: the buzz of customers.

"So what inspired you to become an IRONMAN?" JJ asked Charlie as he turned over the "closed" sign and locked the front door.

"It's something I've wanted to do for about fifteen years, ever since I really started running long distance," Charlie said. "I promised myself I would do an IRONMAN before I was thirty-five, so here I am."

"That's as good a reason as any." JJ cleared a spot on the counter and pulled up another stool for Charlie. "Alright, so let's get into it. As I mentioned at the track, today is about figuring out how to get you where you need to be when you get to the start line in twenty weeks. After coaching for so long, I've found that doing a quick questionnaire-type pulse-check is really valuable to get a sense of where you are now. Do you mind if we start there?"

"Go for it," Charlie said, smiling. "You're the boss."

JJ launched in. "You mentioned you've done some triathlons before, right? Tell me about that."

"Well, when I was in college, I did the shorter sprint-distance triathlon races down the coast."

"Awesome. What was your best result?"

"I came in third in the state championships when I was nineteen. But I think that had less to do with my bike splits and more to do with the fact that only four people turned up on race day," Charlie joked.

For the next thirty minutes, JJ quizzed Charlie about this goals, personal best times, and current fitness levels. It turned out Charlie was a solid swimmer and runner, having been on the swim team all through his school years and, more recently, completing a couple of marathons in just under four hours. "Cycling is probably my weakest leg," Charlie admitted. "Except for those early sprint triathlons, I've never really cycled competitively or for long distances."

"That's no problem," JJ said as he reviewed the first three pages of questions. "You're starting from a great base level of fitness, so we'll get you there. Just one more question and I can get started on your training program. How much time and flexibility do you have to fit in all the required training?"

"As much as is required," Charlie responded enthusiastically. "This is my number-one priority for the next twenty weeks, so whatever you need me to do to get race-ready, I'm there."

JJ nodded. "That's great, but I need to know *exactly* how many hours I can allocate for your training. Can you do fifteen hours a week? Twenty? Thirty? Can I have you for six hours on a Sunday, for example?" He asked this realizing what a ridiculous commitment that would be, especially for a fellow entrepreneur.

"Seriously, JJ. Whatever is needed. I can arrange my schedule to be as flexible as necessary."

JJ looked incredulous. "Really? Don't you run, like, a bunch of companies?" He hadn't meant to blurt this out, but he was legitimately shocked. "Sorry. I often do a little internet stalking on my new trainees, so I read a bit about your background. Seriously, dude, how on earth can you fit in ten hours for training, let alone say you're totally flexible?"

"Well, these days, I find I don't need to spend as much time in the office as I used to when I was starting out," Charlie said.

"Wow, that must be nice," JJ said, feeling envious and, frankly, a little depressed. "I'm pulled in so many different directions between running the shop, dealing with sales reps, my accountant, the landlord, barely keeping up with accounts payable, overseeing the training squad, I feel like I'm working twenty-seven hours a day. And that doesn't even include spending time with my wife and kids."

He broke off, suddenly embarrassed by how candid he was being with a complete stranger. He looked at Charlie, who appeared to be listening closely, which JJ interpreted as an invitation to continue. "Sometimes I feel like a Vaudeville plate-spinner," he said, feeling a little relief at being able to vent to someone. "And if one more plate is added to my stack, the whole thing will come crashing down. I know if Cadence were just twice as profitable, life would be a whole lot easier."

Charlie looked thoughtful. "It's twenty weeks till my IRONMAN, right?" he asked.

"Yeah."

"You should be able to double your profits in that time."

JJ looked at him indignantly. "What? In only twenty weeks?"

"Absolutely. I know five months might not sound like a lot of time, but I've seen it happen time and time again—often faster! And I've worked with a lot of business owners. For that matter, I could turn the question around and ask you: Only twenty weeks? To get me IRONMAN ready? When I haven't exercised really hard in the last few years and can barely bike up a hill without fainting?"

"If you follow the plan and do the work, I can get you there," JJ said. At least he was confident about his coaching abilities.

"Exactly." Charlie smiled as though he'd made his point clear, but JJ didn't follow. Instead of explaining himself, Charlie turned the conversation back to the store. "Tell me about your strategy or framework. What are you doing to grow the business?"

"Well," JJ said, "we've had a guy doing SEO to get the website to appear at the top of searches for the term 'bike store.' We've done some magazine and local newspaper advertising to increase awareness, and we've sponsored some of the local competitions. We're thinking about…"

"Let me stop you right there," Charlie said. "How are all of those things working out for you?"

JJ wasn't prepared for the question. "Well, uh, I think the advertising makes us more visible to athletes and potential customers than our competitors in the area are. And our search rankings have definitely improved."

"Let me phrase it another way," Charlie said. "Have any of the things you've just mentioned increased your sales?"

JJ froze. He hadn't really been keeping track, though based on the number of customers he'd had lately, he guessed the correct answer was, "Not really."

"JJ, do you know the difference between tactics and strategy?" Charlie asked, taking the pressure off JJ even if just for a second.

"Umm...strategy is above the shoulders; tactics are below?" JJ joked raising his eyebrows.

Charlie laughed. "I like it. I'm stealing that one. But back to my point. SEO, magazine ads, sponsorship—all those things sound sexy, but they're just *tactics*—things anyone can do to try and drum up sales. Without an underlying strategy or framework behind them, though, they won't get you very far. You need to understand *why* you're doing them."

He paused for a moment as JJ let his words sink in.

"Think of it this way," Charlie continued. "I, just like any of the athletes you coach, can jump on YouTube or a blog and find heaps of cycling tips, running programs, or swim workouts, right?"

"Sure," JJ replied, not sure where Charlie was going with this.

"If I started doing them randomly—a swim session here, a long ride there—would that get me across the IRONMAN finish line?"

JJ waited for him to continue.

"Of course not! We come to you to help us put it all together, to make sure we are not too focused on one leg of the race, one discipline. We need a complete, overall training and race strategy of which each individual component and training session is just one part. Sure the internet does a great job of making all those business tactics über sexy and convincing you why they're important, but without an underlying strategy or framework, you'll never make it to the finish line."

Understanding flickered in JJ's eyes. "Go on," he said, leaning forward on the shop counter.

"The way I look at it, tactics might generate some cash, but strategy creates profit. That newspaper ad or widely shared Facebook post might get you an extra sale here or there, but if you want long-term growth, you need a real plan, something much more purposeful and trackable."

"Okay," JJ said, "So what is it?"

"Well, it's like that story you told us the other day about the British cycling coach. The one about how his team used 1% improvements to win the Tour de France. In that case, the coach made a bunch of small improvements across a wide range of areas and it paid off big time, right?"

"Yeah, so?"

"Well, the same applies in business. Except instead of 1% wins over a bunch of different areas, you really only need to make *10% Wins* over seven different areas. It may sound intimidating now, but it's surprisingly easy once you become familiar with and start executing the framework. Just get a *10% Win* in a few key areas and your profits will double. Trust me. How do you think I manage to run multiple businesses simultaneously and still have time to train for an IRONMAN competition?"

The question hung in the air tantalizingly as JJ looked at his watch. The thirty minutes he'd planned to spend with Charlie had somehow turned into fifty and he was going to be late for dinner *again*.

"It's been a long day," JJ said, sighing as he imagined missing Ben and Emily's bedtime. "Why don't we meet again for breakfast in a few days after I've put together your training plan ...and strategy, and you can tell me all about these *10% Wins*?"

"Sure. I'm available," Charlie said.

"Have you ever been to Jerry's Diner, out on East Main? It's a great place to talk business and the food is exceptional. How about we meet there Saturday at 10am?"

"That sounds like a plan," Charlie said. "See you then."

Chapter 3

The Seven Levers

J J waved from a back booth at Jerry's Diner as soon as he saw Charlie's tall form step through the front door.

Charlie smiled and nodded, his long strides covering the distance quickly. He slid into the booth opposite JJ and put his phone on silent before slipping it into his back pocket. *Not only can he take the time to train for an IRONMAN*, JJ thought. *He doesn't have to worry about missing a call.*

"Morning, coach," Charlie said, smiling broadly. "Got my training plan ready?"

"Sure thing. Hey, did I see you out running on the beach yesterday evening, near the pier?" JJ asked.

Charlie looked surprised. "Yeah, that was me. You mean your triathlon coaching comes with twenty-four-hour surveillance too?" he joked.

"That's right—watch your back," JJ gibed. "No, I had dinner with my family on the boardwalk last night, and I thought I saw you jogging along the beachside track, but it was too far to be sure."

"Dinner with the family sounds nice," Charlie said. "What's your wife's name?"

"Sarah. Yours?"

"Chloe," Charlie said. "You'll have to meet her sometime. She's a great girl. We grew up on the same block, if you can believe that. No kids yet, though."

"Oh, I can believe it. Sarah was my high-school sweetheart."

"No kidding? That's great. I'm still amazed Chloe has been able to tolerate me for so long! Perhaps, when training slows down, we can arrange for a double date?"

"Sarah would love that!" JJ said. "Plus, I usually like to take my IRONMAN trainees out for dinner a couple of weeks before race day. It's a little reward for all of the hard work they put in to get there."

"You guys ready to order?" The redheaded waitress seemed to appear out of nowhere, pen poised over her order pad.

After they placed their orders, JJ pulled a laminated spreadsheet out of his bag and set it on the table. "Here's the detailed version of your custom training schedule for the next eight weeks," he said. "Don't worry, I've emailed it to you too, in an easier format. I'm just a little old-school about having a hard copy. Plus you can take it to your pool sessions without worry."

"Yeah, I can see that," Charlie said, grinning at the shiny laminate.

They spent the next twenty minutes going over the training schedule. It was grueling: four group sessions plus four solo sessions a week, with only one day of rest. In his first week alone, Charlie would be doing three hours of swimming, three-and-a-half hours of running and seven hours of riding, plus ice baths and massages when he could.

"Don't plan to take it easy on me, huh coach?"

"That's what I said, isn't it?" JJ countered.

"You're nothing if not honest," Charlie said as the waitress brought over their orders.

"I'm extremely curious about this *10% Wins* idea you mentioned the other night," JJ said as he dug into his veggie omelet.

"Alright, let's have a crack at it," Charlie said as he took a bite of his scrambled eggs. He took a sip of his coffee and leaned back against the booth. "The idea is actually very simple. I have come to realize that there are only seven things that really drive any business profits, and once you identify them, increasing them each by just 10% will double your business profits. So getting seven *10% Wins*, as I call them, in twenty weeks should be pretty easy."

"So you were serious the other day when you said seven steps," JJ said. "Why is it that everything seems to be seven something: seven habits, seven sins, seven dwarves?"

"Never thought about it that way," Charlie said, shrugging his shoulders. "It's a lucky number I guess. And, more importantly, it's what I've found to be true. For example, back when I was in college, doing those sprint-distance triathlons, I worked at an athletic shoe store. I realize selling shoes and selling bikes are not exactly the same, but they have certain things in common, so I think it will serve to illustrate my point."

"I'm all ears," JJ said, leaning forward so as not to miss a word of what Charlie was about to tell him.

"The first element of any business is traffic. In the shoe store, traffic was all about how many people walked into the store. Like every business, but especially in retail, not everyone who walked in the door really wanted to purchase a pair of shoes. So I call all this foot traffic, or people, **Suspects**."

JJ pulled a notebook and pen out of his bag and began to take notes. "Go on," he told Charlie.

"As sales staff, our main focus was getting as many of those Suspects to try on a pair of running shoes as possible. Certainly some of them had walked in intending to buy shoes, but others might be convinced to make a purchase if they found something they liked.

"To do that, in our case, they'd need to try on a pair of shoes. These people would be what I call **Prospects** because, by sitting down and trying on a pair of shoes, they had shown they were a little more serious about buying something. This opened up a window through which the other sales people and I could sell to them, making them more likely prospective clients."

JJ scribbled *Suspects and Prospects* into his notebook.

"Obviously, the number of those people who ended up buying was the most important factor," Charlie continued. "Those are called **Conversions**."

"So Suspects are the people who walk into your store, visit your website, or call your company sales team," JJ said, trying to make sure he understood. "Those who show serious interest and opt in to be sold to are your Prospects. Then the percentage of people who end up buying from you is your Conversion rate?"

"Exactly," Charlie said. "Next, when it comes to the revenues and profits of any business, it's important to know what the **Average Item Price** is, so for us it was knowing the average price for the products we sold—shoes, socks, insoles, etc."

"All of us sales staff were also rewarded based on the number of items we were able to sell to each customer. For example, we were taught to always try to sell a pair of socks, a replacement pair of insoles, or shoe cleaner to every person who bought a pair of shoes.

That's known as your **Items per Sale**." Charlie said as JJ continued to take notes.

"And although we didn't do this at the shoe store, something I've learned over the years with my own businesses is the importance of getting people to come back and buy again, increasing the **Transactions per Customer**. See, the typical pair of running shoes only lasts about 300 to 500 miles, so if we had been more proactive about educating and marketing to our existing customers, I'm sure we could have sold more shoes to them over time."

Charlie paused to make sure his words were sinking in. JJ gestured for him to go on.

"And, finally, profit is all about how much money you keep in your pocket at the end of the day, so your **Margins**—the difference between how much revenue you bring in and how much you have to pay to suppliers, employees, etc.—play a big factor in all of this. The better your Margins, the higher your profits."

JJ looked down at what he had written in his notebook so far.

THE 7 LEVERS DEFINED

SUSPECTS = Everyone who comes into contact with our business

PROSPECTS = The % of suspects who raise their hands and qualify to be sold to

CONVERSIONS = The % of prospects who actually buy and become customers

AVERAGE ITEM PRICE = The average price of the stuff we sell

ITEMS PER SALE = The # of different items people typically purchase in an individual sale

TRANSACTIONS PER CUSTOMER = How often customers come back and buy again

MARGINS = The amount of profit we make after paying for all expenses

"That all makes sense. Actually, it's kind of obvious when you think about it," JJ said. "But how does this double your profits?"

"Can I borrow your notebook and pen for a minute?" Charlie asked. JJ slid the book over to his side of the table.

"Let's crunch some numbers, shall we?" Charlie grinned as he flipped to a clean page and began to write. "Let's say the shoe store had foot traffic of 1,000 Suspects a month," Charlie said as he wrote 'Suspects: 1,000' on the page. "And of those 1,000 people, 600 opted in and tried on a pair of shoes. That's a Prospect rate of 60%. If 40% of those prospects who tried on a pair of shoes bought them, that's 240 sales, or a 40% Conversion rate.

"Now let's say the Average Item Price of products was $100," Charlie said as he wrote the figure down.

"Those are some pretty expensive socks," JJ observed.

"Well, remember we are looking at Average Item Price here," Charlie clarified. "A typical pair of quality running shoes is about $180 and socks are like $20, so across the store's entire range, the average item price was about $100."

"Ah, okay. Just like the best racing bikes cost a few thousand dollars but other gear like helmets, water bottles, and bike shorts are much less expensive."

"Precisely," Charlie paused as he took a sip of his coffee. "Getting back to the calculation, let's say one in every five people bought two items—a pair of shoes and a pair of socks, for example. Then we have an Items per Sale figure of 1.2." He wrote this figure down in JJ's notebook. "Let's also say that one in ten people came back at some later date and bought another pair of shoes; that's 1.1 Transactions per Customer. So if the shoe store worked on a total Margin of say 30%, this would result in a profit for the business of $9,504 for the month." Charlie finished writing and spun the notebook around for JJ to see.

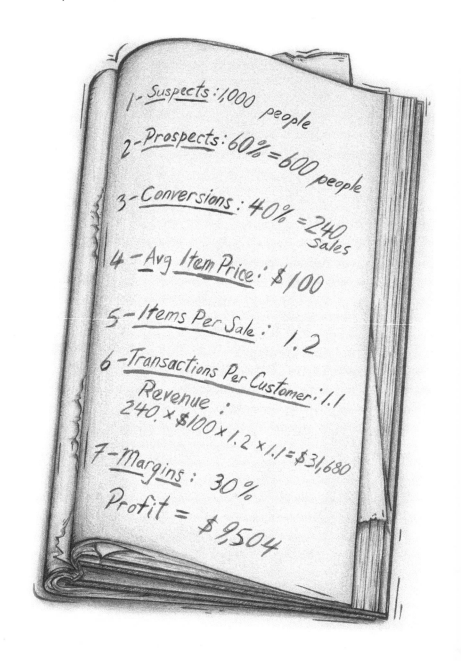

1- <u>Suspects</u>: 1,000 people

2- <u>Prospects</u>: 60% = 600 people

3- <u>Conversions</u>: 40% = 240 sales

4- <u>Avg Item Price</u>: $100

5- <u>Items Per Sale</u>: 1.2

6- <u>Transactions Per Customer</u>: 1.1

Revenue:
240 × $100 × 1.2 × 1.1 = $31,680

7- <u>Margins</u>: 30%

Profit = $9,504

"So if the average client spent $100 per item and bought 1.2 items each purchase," JJ reasoned, "then a typical sale was about $120 in total?"

"Spot on," Charlie said.

"Cool. So if the store made 240 sales at $120, but clients came back an average of 1.1 times, the store's total revenue would have been $31,680," said JJ, happy to see his mental math match the scratching Charlie had made.

"And when you factor in the store's margin of 30 percent, the profits would have been $9,504 for the month," Charlie explained. "Now let's see what happens when we have a few *10% Wins* and increase each of these seven areas by just 10%." Charlie pulled the notebook back to his side of the booth and continued scribbling.

"The shoe store owner does a little marketing and the foot traffic goes from 1,000 people to 1,100," Charlie said as he wrote "Suspects 1,100" on the new page. "You get better at engaging those people and increase the percentage of Prospects who try on a pair of shoes from 60% to 66%—another small 10% increase. With a little salesmanship, the store increases the percentage of Conversions from 40% to 44%. That's now 319 odd customers, up from 240. So far, are these *10% Wins* looking scary or unrealistic?" Charlie asked, pausing to make sure JJ understood the math.

JJ stared at the calculations for a moment. "Going from 240 paying customers to 319 kind of does seem scary. But getting those three *10% Wins* doesn't seem unrealistic at all."

"Totally agree," Charlie said. "Having a framework to work with in your business makes this so much easier. In fact, if you didn't get the wins with your Prospects and Conversions as well, you would have had to increase your traffic by one third, just to get the same 319 sales. So, what's easier: three small *10% Wins* in different areas, or having to increase one area, like the traffic of your business, by an entire third?"

Charlie didn't wait for JJ's response. "Let's keep going. Say the improved salesmanship not only increased Conversions but also resulted in more sales of higher-priced products, from $100 to $110 on average. And the team started to suggest socks and insoles more often."

"Like McDonald's—would you like fries with that?" JJ added.

"Yeah, exactly like that," Charlie said with a grin. That phrase might be the most overused example in the history of business, but he was still pleased JJ was beginning to understand.

He continued. "Let's say that question also results in a *10% Win*, taking the Items per Sale from 1.2 to 1.32. And with a little bit of marketing creativity, the store is able to get people back more often to replace their shoes sooner, taking the Transactions per Customer rate from 1.1 to 1.21. And, finally, by taking a look at the entire business, eliminating waste and negotiating a little with suppliers, we take the shoe store's Margins from 30% to 33%. Where do you think the store's profits are now?" asked Charlie before handing over the new figures.

JJ cleared his throat. "Well, given where this whole conversation is going, I have to say doubled, right? But it does blow my mind that just 10% increases can do that."

Charlie nodded. "Yeah, just seven easy *10% Wins* and we've taken the shoe store's profits from $9,504 to $18,495. Essentially doubled." He set the pen down and waited for JJ's reaction.

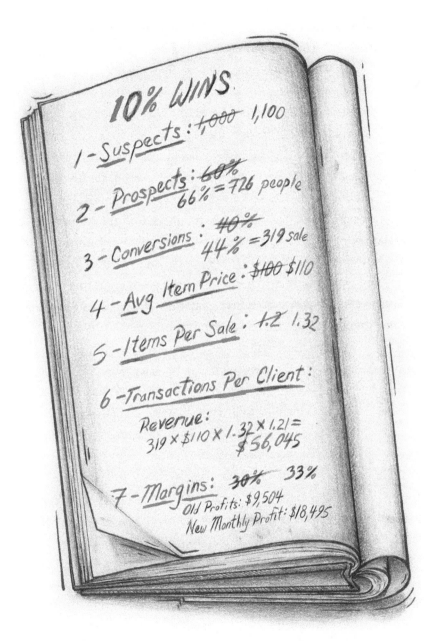

10% WINS
1 - Suspects: ~~1,000~~ 1,100
2 - Prospects: ~~60%~~
        66% = 726 people
3 - Conversions: ~~40%~~
        44% = 319 sale
4 - Avg Item Price: ~~$100~~ $110
5 - Items Per Sale: ~~1.2~~ 1.32
6 - Transactions Per Client:
        Revenue:
        319 × $110 × 1.32 × 1.21 =
                $56,045
7 - Margins: ~~30%~~ 33%
        Old Profits: $9,504
        New Monthly Profit: $18,495

JJ collected his thoughts. "This *10% Win* thing seems great, but it feels too simple. There has to be more to a successful business than a series of *10% Wins*. I mean, they charge like $80,000 for a two-year MBA."

Charlie leaned forward on the table. "Let me tell you a quick story." He took another sip of coffee before he began. JJ also couldn't help but wonder if Charlie was pausing for dramatic effect. "A few years ago, my business partners and I owned an e-commerce business that was having serious problems with the warehouse and distribution company that handled its products. End clients had started complaining to our company that they were receiving empty boxes from the warehouse instead of the products they ordered. Obviously, something was going terribly wrong on the production line and was costing everyone—the e-commerce business, the warehouse, and the clients—money, goodwill, and a lot of time.

"The management team at the warehouse company decided to hire an expensive outside consultant to solve the problem. This expert advisor had everything you'd expect him to have: an impressive website, a large social media following, an MBA from a top university. He'd even written an online course on warehousing secrets that he sold to businesses all over the globe.

"He personally worked on the warehouse project for six weeks, during which time he designed a sophisticated system with precision scales that would weigh each box coming off the pick-and-pack line. If the box weighed less than it should, a bell would ring, the line would stop, and the shift supervisor would walk over and remove the empty box. He'd pass it back to the team so they could repack correctly and press another button when done to restart the line.

"The CEO of the warehouse company was very satisfied with the return on investment statistics for the project and even passed them onto us clients to reassure us of the great lengths they were going to in order to solve the problem. Not a single empty box left the warehouse after the new system was put in place."

As Charlie paused to take another sip of coffee, JJ spoke up. "Okay," he said, a little confused by the point of the story. "But what does that have to do with me?"

"Well, a week later, the CEO read the new weekly statistics report," Charlie said. "He was confused. According to the statistics, the fancy new system they'd put in place had picked up zero boxes that week when it should have been picking up at least a dozen a day. Could the report be wrong? Or was the expensive system broken already?"

JJ knew the questions were rhetorical; he waited for Charlie to go on.

"The consultant and his team of experts took some time to investigate and came back saying the report was correct. The scales weren't picking up any defects because *all boxes* that got to that point in the conveyor belt were packed with the correct order inside.

"Even more puzzled now, the CEO went to the factory and approached the precision scales. Close to the scale, he noticed a big cheap plastic desk fan that was blowing any empty boxes off the belt into a bin. Every hour, one of the team members would take all the empty boxes out of the bin to the back of the line for repacking. 'What is this?' the CEO asked. 'Oh, that,' said one of the workers. 'Just a fan. Tony put it there 'cause he was getting tired of coming down to the line every time the bloody bell rang.'"

Charlie finished his story with a look of satisfaction on his face. He took another large bite of his eggs and called the waitress over for a refill on his coffee.

Meanwhile, JJ puzzled over the moral of the story. "So what you're saying is, I might have been making this whole business thing too complicated?"

"Exactly," Charlie said grinning. "It's not about spending a bunch of money or putting in a ton of effort to pull off some miracle feat. It's about how *effective* your strategy is over the long-run."

Most budding IRONMAN athletes fell into the same trap, JJ thought to himself. The idea of completing over 130 miles in a single day seems near impossible, but as JJ knew all too well, breaking the training down into "single-session successes" was what got people over the finish line.

"You've given me a lot to think about," JJ said. "If I can achieve even half of those levers in the next twenty weeks, I'll take that as a win."

"Why not think bigger?" Charlie said. "I'll make a deal with you: you get me IRONMAN-ready in twenty weeks, and I'll coach you to seven *10% Wins* in the same timeframe."

A smile stretched across JJ's face. "Deal."

Shaking hands on it, the two men paid their check and agreed to meet again at the next training session—a group ride scheduled for early the following week.

As JJ slipped behind the wheel of his Jeep, he felt a little less stressed—and even a little hopeful. Maybe there was something to this *10% Win* thing after all.

---

7 Levers Calculator Online
Want to see the effect of 10% Wins in various situations?
Want to discover what a 10% Win will do for your business?
Visit the online interactive calculator at
www.cadencebook.com/extra

Chapter 4

10% Wins

_____

The following Monday morning, JJ headed to the track for another squad session. He was especially looking forward to seeing Charlie, as he'd spent the weekend thinking about their conversation at Jerry's a few days prior. He'd felt good after he left the diner, but the more he thought about the *7 Levers*, the more skeptical he became that they could actually work the way Charlie promised. He'd read dozens of books on sales, marketing, and entrepreneurship, each of which promised to hold the key to outstanding growth. He'd tried it all and was still floundering. He trusted Charlie because he was clearly successful, but surely there must have been more to his meteoric rise than these *7 Levers*? He was determined to find out what Charlie wasn't telling him.

After sending most of the students off on an easy recovery ride, JJ held Charlie back for a one-on-one ride over slightly rougher terrain.

"Hey, champ, we're gonna push ourselves a little harder than the rest of the group, so I thought we'd head out on a different loop today."

"Sure thing, coach," Charlie said amiably.

The two men mounted their bikes and quickly settled into a brisk training pace as they peddled off down the road. Chitchat flowed easily; they talked about their work and their families, but before long, JJ felt compelled to steer the conversation back to the *7 Levers*. "You saw the number in your notebook," Charlie said after JJ had expressed his doubts. "It's just math."

"Sure, mathematically the hypothetical numbers you showed me make sense, but we live in the real world," JJ countered. "It can't possibly be that easy to achieve all those *10% Wins*."

Sensing the need for a real-world illustration, Charlie continued. "Let me tell you about my accountant and how he's applied this framework to his own practice."

"You sure have a lot of stories," JJ joked. "I'm all ears."

"See, my accountant, Don, although amazing with a spreadsheet, wasn't the most imaginative or outgoing entrepreneur you'd ever met," Charlie began. "He ran a great little practice, serving the local business community for decades, but when his son graduated from college and wanted to join the firm so he could one day take over the family business, Don knew he needed to drum up some more clients. Up until that point all of Don's clients had been lifers, and the only growth he had was from the odd referral; he simply wasn't doing enough business to keep his son busy."

"Sounds like a lot of people I know," JJ said. "My wife, Sarah, is actually an accountant—part-time at the moment—and gets most of her clients through referrals."

"And that's fine," Charlie said, "if you're not trying to grow your business. The problem for Don was that his growth was not really in his control. That worked for decades, as he was happy to grow slowly, trading his time for an hourly fee, but when he decided to grow the business to accommodate his son, it wasn't enough. He had to make changes quickly to provide enough work for both of them."

Charlie paused as he and JJ made their way up a particularly steep hill. Once he caught his breath, he continued. "At this point I'd been lucky enough to have some success with a couple of businesses in different markets, and, being my accountant, Don had been along for the *ride*," Charlie said.

JJ rolled his eyes at Charlie's terrible pun as he peddled beside him.

"Anyway, Don called me one afternoon saying, 'Charlie, I need to see you as soon as possible. We've got a problem I need to talk to you about.' Now I'm not sure if you've ever received a voicemail like that," Charlie said, "but it's not what you want to hear from the man looking after your books."

"You've got that right!" JJ's laugh was genuine but he still couldn't help feel a little queasy at the thought of the many uncomfortable conversations he'd been having with his own accountant recently.

"Of course, the problem had nothing to do with my balance sheet and everything to do with the lack of work Don had to give his son. Don had called me because he knew my partners and I had bought an e-commerce business fourteen months earlier—the same one I told you about the other day, actually—and had increased its bottom line significantly by focusing strategically on the areas of the business that generated profit."

JJ could tell Charlie was finding it more and more difficult to tell his story as he exerted himself on the bike, but his trainee continued without complaint. "Don wanted to know what we did to get growth like that and asked if I could help him do something similar with his accounting practice. It wasn't really until I started helping Don that I realized my process of making companies more profitable was actually a pretty straightforward strategy. And that's when the *7 Levers* framework was born."

"I'm going to stop you right there, Charlie," JJ interrupted. "I definitely want to hear the end of this story, but right now we've got an IRONMAN to prepare for." With that, JJ got down on his bike's aerobars and sped off in the distance as Charlie did his best to keep up.

* * * * *

"That was pretty solid for a newbie," JJ said after he and Charlie had reached the end of the road.

"Thanks…coach," Charlie said, clearly winded from the effort.

"So what happened with Don?" JJ asked.

Charlie gave a lighthearted smirk as he tried to catch his breath. He had never ridden that hard before, and JJ knew it.

"Okay, okay," JJ said. "Fair enough. I'll give you a few minutes to get yourself together. Why don't we find an easier place to recover?" JJ turned the corner leading Charlie to a less busy road which was more suitable for a leisurely recovery ride.

In between a few puffs, Charlie explained what he, Don, and Don's son had done to get their *10% Wins.*

"First we needed to build the awareness of Don's practice, increasing their Suspects and generating new traffic," Charlie said. "All we did was create a small but targeted Google AdWords campaign. It was the low-hanging fruit. If someone is in need of a new accountant, they go to Google and search. So we just went where the predisposed buyers were. No one searches for an accountant for the fun of it," he added.

"That's for sure," JJ agreed.

"We set a low budget, crafted some appealing advertising copy, and made it so the advertisements would only show to people within a thirty-mile radius of the business. After that, we turned to the next lever. Don had always offered new prospective clients a free thirty-minute meeting before they officially signed on with him. So we just jazzed it up a bit by giving it a name—"Actionable Accounting Audit"—and promising potential clients that Don would try to find $1,000 of savings or deductions to prove himself worthy of their business. By encouraging everyone who visited his website or called the office to opt in for this free assessment, we were able to quickly identify Prospects because only qualified leads—those serious Suspects interested in hiring Don—would self-select to participate."

"Seems simple enough," JJ said.

"Next, to help Don convert as many of these Actionable Accounting Audit Prospects as possible, we put together a checklist of sorts for him to follow during the sessions to lead people to buy his services. Before the structure, Don would often just give so much free advice he'd end up talking potential clients out of the sale. A little structure, some basic results-in-advance selling, and Don's charm worked like a treat," Charlie said.

"Probably the coolest concept that Don implemented during all this was an idea proposed by his son, Thomas. Doing a tax return is a pretty straightforward and finite service, so Don wasn't sure how to increase Items per Sale. Then Thomas suggested selling air."

"Air?" JJ interjected. "I've heard of tourists buying bottled air from the Australian Outback as a novelty gift, but what are you talking about?"

"Okay, maybe "air" isn't the right word," Charlie said. "Let's say Don and Thomas began to sell "peace of mind". See, a lot of people get nervous that the tax office might audit their accounts, especially since the technology used to analyze anomalies keeps getting better. So Thomas suggested selling a form of audit insurance that would entitle the client to Don's help in the event they were audited. The insurance was much less expensive than what it would cost to hire Don at his hourly rate for the same service, so clients were incentivized to buy the insurance upfront, thus increasing the Items per Sale."

"What about getting them to come back and buy again?" asked JJ. "You only do one tax return a year."

"Too right," said Charlie, "but there are a whole bunch of other services a trusted advisor like Don can provide—tax planning, certain investment advice, etc. The problem was he had never been that proactive in offering them to his clients. He began to structure pre-planning sessions with all his clients, showing them how a one-hour billable session prior to the end of the fiscal year would save the clients hundreds in taxes."

"Sarah's complained about that before," JJ said. "She always gets frustrated knowing that she could have saved a client thousands of dollars if they had come to her to help plan for the year."

"Totally," agreed Charlie. "That was Don's biggest bugbear too, but we switched it up and turned it into a little profit lever for him."

"Prior Preparation Prevents Piss-Poor Performance," JJ said, echoing one of his favorite coaching phrases.

"More like Prior Preparation Prevents Piss-Poor *Profits*," joked Charlie as he and JJ paused next to a small flower garden where a park groundskeeper was watering the beautiful patch of color.

"Meanwhile," Charlie said, picking up his story, "Don had been running his business like a gardener with an overgrown lawn. He'd spent so much time analyzing everyone else's P&Ls and looking for hidden opportunities to save them some dough that he'd forgotten to look at his own. So one of the first things Thomas did when we started looking for *10% Wins* was to go through the firm's own internal expenses to see where they could decrease costs and increase margins. It took Thomas less than half a day and six phone calls to find an 8% gain in their Margins by eliminating waste, reviewing various agreements, and negotiating others. For example, the cost of the firm's internet package alone was reduced by 22% a month simply by calling the provider and switching to a cheaper plan designed specifically for small businesses."

"What about increasing his Average Item Price?" asked JJ. "You didn't say what Don did to increase that lever."

"Oh, he increased his prices," Charlie responded.

"Yeah, I get that," said JJ. "But what did he *do*?"

"He increased his prices by 10%," Charlie said, grinning. "Don had been doing a fantastic job for clients for years, but he hadn't changed his pricing schedule in a decade. So he simply raised his prices. Now I know not everyone can just increase prices, but guess what happened at the end of all this?"

"He doubled his profits?" JJ said.

"Yes, but he didn't double his workload," Charlie sighed exaggeratedly as if he was breaking terrible news. "The compounded results of the *10% Wins* resulted in his bottom-line profits doubling, but, unfortunately, it didn't double the number of clients he had or the work required to service them." Charlie shook his head as he looked at JJ with a sly grin.

JJ waited for Charlie to continue, but he realized his trainee was trying to get a rise out of him by dragging this story out. "Okay, I'll bite," JJ relented. "How is doubling profits without doubling workload a problem? That's what I want. I can't work twice as hard in the store!"

"For you, absolutely," Charlie said. "It all comes down to knowing your goals. Remember, Don originally wanted to grow his business so he had enough work for his son. What we discovered was that *10%*

Wins in those seven key areas created massive leverage, hence the term *7 Levers*. Don had easily and very quickly doubled his business from a profit perspective but hadn't actually doubled the clients, so his son was still under-utilized in the firm."

"Oh right, of course!" JJ exclaimed, finally getting it. "If you've got spare capacity, that's just profit waiting to be mined. If you've got a machine that manufactures widgets only operating at 50% capacity, it's a wasted resource. So in Don's case, his son's capacity was still being wasted, and that was still a problem."

Charlie glanced over at him and nodded, impressed.

"So what happened?" JJ asked.

"Don and his son just cycled through the *7 Levers* again, working on each area for two weeks in an effort to get another set of *10% Wins*," Charlie said. "He doubled his profits again, over the next fourteen weeks, and increased his client base in the process, which began to make his son busy."

"So he just kept *cycling*," JJ said, realizing Charlie's puns actually had a deeper meaning now. "Well, that's what you need to do—one hour left in the session, eight-minute efforts at 200 watts, two-minute recovery just spinning your legs. Let's go!"

Chapter 5

Just Keep Cycling

"Just keep cycling," JJ said.

"What was that?" Charlie asked, clearly confused as he got out of the pool. The entire squad had just completed their first time-trial of the season—a 1000m effort in the water. For some athletes training for the shorter local events, a 1000m swim seemed like an eternity, but for others like Charlie, it was only about a quarter of the 3.8 km they'd face on race day. But no matter what event they'd be doing during the season, every time trial hurt. It was a chance for them to see the results and rewards of their training, and for coach JJ to see if they were on target with the goals and program. Charlie was in a good starting place, but JJ knew he had a long way to go over the next few months.

"The other day, you said Don cycled through the *7 Levers* with his son again and again," JJ said while Charlie caught his breath and dried off.

"Ah, right," replied Charlie. "Let me shower up and we'll grab one of those terrible coffees from the cafeteria to talk more about that. You got time?"

"Yeah, Matt is opening up today, so I'm good," JJ said with a huge, thankful grin on his face. He was hoping Charlie would offer to impart more wisdom on him today. The story about Don had really convinced him that there was something to this *7 Levers* idea. Now he just needed to know how to put the ideas into action at Cadence.

* * * * *

"So where do I actually start?" JJ asked as he and Charlie settled into a table with their coffees in hand. "I pretty much get the whole *10% Win* idea, but how do I actually figure out how to execute them?"

"Excellent question, and believe it or not, I have a process for that, too," Charlie said.

"I believe it," JJ said with a laugh.

JJ reached into his gym bag, pulled out his tattered notebook, and immediately turned it over to Charlie. Charlie flipped to a blank page and wrote:

"The first thing you need to do is **Clarify** what each lever is for you. In other words, you need to define what the *7 Levers* look like for your business." Charlie turned the notebook around so JJ could see the list. "Every business is different, and only after you have clarity on what each lever is for your business model can you even begin to start working on those *10% Wins* strategically."

"That makes sense," said JJ. "I've actually been thinking about that, and I think I have a pretty good sense of what most of them mean for a retail business like mine thanks to your shoe store example. But Suspects and Prospects—that's where I trip up. Isn't everyone who walks into the store a potential customer? Aren't they all Prospects?"

Charlie took a long sip of his coffee and grimaced slightly at the bitter taste before answering; the stuff really wasn't great, but at least it provided a little pick-me-up after a tough workout. "Well not always. How many times have you walked into a store just to kill some time while your wife was shopping at the mall? Or sat on the couch browsing online bike stores with no intention at all to purchase?"

"Well, yeah lots of times," JJ said. "But isn't the job of the sales team to convince that person to buy something?"

"Slow down there, champ. You need to romance a girl a little first," Charlie said, laughing at his own joke. "Taking the time to really differentiate between Suspects and Prospects is something a lot of business owners don't ever think about. Not every person who walks into your store, visits your website, or inquires about your service is going to buy—from you, from a competitor, or even at all. But for the ones who will, they will almost *always* take some sort of definable action *before* purchasing. That action shows you that they are 'self-selecting' and are truly interested in your product or service. And this action almost always changes the direction and tone of conversation. The way you talk to a Suspect is actually very different from how you talk to a Prospect."

"Okay, but what is that action?" JJ could feel himself growing impatient, but he knew it was just because he was anxious to get started.

"It could be a lot of different things. There may be lots of small steps, but typically there is one *big* step, like providing enough information to receive a personalized quote, taking the time to try on a pair of shoes, signing up for a free trial of your product, or providing an email address to receive a free report on your website. You want to clarify what that specific qualifying action is because that is what makes a Prospect a Prospect.

"Let me ask you this question," Charlie continued noticing JJ's confused face. "When you first opened Cadence, you obviously used a tradesman to help do the shop fit-out and carpentry, right?"

"Sure did," replied JJ lifting his palms towards Charlie "These soft puppies haven't done a day of manual labor in their life."

"Haha. Whatever you say, coach! So when you were calling around to find the right tradesman, you were essentially a Suspect to each and every one, right?"

"Yeah," JJ said.

"So let me ask you this: what action did you take or information did you request to show you were a true Prospect to a specific tradesman?"

"Well, I guess I agreed for them to come out and give me a personalized quote," JJ replied with a little more confidence.

"Now think back to the conversations you had with that tradesman. Was the conversation leading up to the quote different from the one you had after you received the quote?"

JJ considered the question. "Well, yeah, come to think of it, it was. Before I received the quote, the conversation was much more general, and they offered few specifics. But as soon as I got the quote, they started selling me a little harder, giving me a bunch of different options and ideas based on my specific goals."

"Right," Charlie said. "Whether the tradesman was conscious of what he was doing or not, he knew you were serious about doing business with him and was therefore more ready to engage."

JJ considered the story Charlie had told about Prospects trying on shoes at the shoe store and thought about what the equivalent of that would be for his business.

"What is it that Prospects do to self-select and show they are *really*, *seriously*, interested in buying from you at Cadence?" Charlie asked, as if reading JJ's thoughts. "What action do you *want* them to take to show this interest and become a Prospect?"

JJ paused for a moment and thought about various times in his own life when he had "self-selected" and demonstrated he was a real Prospect. In addition to the time he requested a quote from the shop fitter, he remembered once when he was searching the internet for an online accounting package for the store and signed up for a free trial to test it out before buying. He also thought back to the many hours he'd spent online researching marketing and business tips as he tried to open and then grow Cadence. Although he'd visited a ton of websites, making him a Suspect, he only subscribed to a select few free newsletters. He still got several of those newsletters, indicating that the company clearly saw him as a Prospect for a more expensive package or service.

"Essentially, you can't work on leveraging what you haven't labeled and clarified," Charlie said, interrupting JJ's stream of consciousness.

"'You can't leverage what you don't label,' I like that," said JJ as he wrote it at the bottom of the page. He looked back to the list Charlie had written down. "What's next? **Capture**?"

"Yup," Charlie said. "Once you've clarified each of the *7 Levers*, you need to Capture information on what you're already doing in these areas—even if it's unconscious currently. For example, are you currently engaging in any advertising or marketing efforts to draw more Suspects to the store or website? Do you have anything in place to help identify Prospects—like an optional email list or a free trial service? Have your employees been trained to ask 'Would you like fries with that?' or does your website have a function that recommends similar or complementary products to people when they put something in their cart or make a purchase? Once you've identified what you're *already* doing in these *7 Levers*, you can move onto the next step of the process."

"**Calculate**," JJ said, reading the third bullet point in his notebook."

"Exactly! Just like that pain you put us through this morning," joked Charlie. "You need to take a pulse check of where you are right now. How many Suspects are coming into the store? What is the Average Item Price and average number of Items per Sale? I don't think I need to explain to you the importance of keeping track of progress, do I, *coach*?" Charlie said.

"I always say, I can't coach what we don't count," JJ said.

"This is business, mate," Charlie corrected. "'You can't *manage*, what you don't *measure*.' It's a bit of a cliché now in business, but it's true."

"Got it," JJ replied as he wrote that down in his notebook. "Though, I have to admit, I'm not terribly excited about doing this math for Cadence right now. I'm sure our numbers are probably worse than I think they are."

"Maybe," Charlie said, pragmatically. "Maybe not. But regardless, you should feel good about taking action. You're just one step closer to having a workable strategy you can put in place to grow your business. If you want to see real results, you've got to deal with real facts."

"Thanks for the pep talk," JJ mocked.

"Anytime!" Charlie grinned. "Now, where were we…Ah, yes! This is the fun part. Once you've Calculated where you currently are, you can **Correct** any anomalies. You'd be surprised at how often business owners think a process is working just fine only to discover the opposite. And taking the time to Correct these problems can result in a quick *10% Win* on its own."

"How so?" JJ asked.

Charlie paused to consider. "Take the classic 'Would you like fries with that?' example you mentioned at our meeting at Jerry's. Even though management has made that part of the standard sales process, if they're not measuring how often people say it, it could easily fall through the cracks. They might assume the frontline employees are asking this question during every transaction when they actually aren't. Suddenly, McDonald's is selling far fewer fries than they could be. They might even conclude that the strategy doesn't work and decide it's not important to continue. When in reality, the strategy works great, it's just not being executed consistently. Or, say you've set up a Google AdWords campaign for your e-commerce business but, somehow, it got turned off without your knowledge. Simply by correcting that problem, you could easily increase that lever by 10%. Trust me…it happens to the best of us." Charlie said with a knowing wink.

"Ah, I got it," JJ said. "My friend Jules, who works at one of my key suppliers, mentioned a few months ago that they recently partnered with a large national sports supply store to run a promotion through the store's website. A rebate offer was supposed to pop up when you clicked on any one of their bikes. A week or so after the promotion started, they realized they hadn't seen a consistent change in sales, so they looked at the site and realized the pop-up wasn't working as it was supposed to. Once they talked to the people who designed the website and fixed the glitch, the promotion worked incredibly well for them. They got something like 15% more sales that month than they had previously."

"Exactly!" Charlie leaned back in his chair, satisfied that his new student was catching on so quickly. "I told you it worked!"

"Okay, I promise not to doubt you anymore!" JJ looked back at his notes. "The next item on the list is **Create**. I assume that's where I Create a new strategy for each of the levers?"

"Bravo!" Charlie said. "Once you've gone through what you're already doing—Capturing, Calculating and Correcting any obvious errors, and banking those quick *10% Wins*, then you can start figuring out new strategies for each of the levers."

"So then I just start from the start? And begin working on the foot traffic to the store. Increasing Suspects, and then Prospects, and then on from there?"

"Well, you *can* start there," explained Charlie. "But I would start with what I call the 'lowest-hanging fruit.' In other words, the areas that will give you the quickest results for relatively little effort."

"The instant results I need are more sales," said JJ, his enthusiasm waning. "And to get more sales, I need more people to sell to."

"Let's ride the brakes a little here," Charlie said with another terrible cycling cliché. "What you need is more *profits*. People, profit, and revenue are three very different things," Charlie explained. "Sales generate revenue, but profits keep the business running. And remember, there are seven drivers of profit—the *7 Levers* we already discussed. Conversions, or *sales*, are just one of those levers. Sure, they're important, but they're only one part of the larger equation. Increasing your foot traffic—your Suspects—by 10% will make the exact same change to your profits as, say, increasing your Items per Sale by 10%. You have people in the store right now, right?" Charlie asked.

"Hopefully," JJ said.

"So the lowest-hanging fruit, and the place I would start implementing the *7 Levers*, is in emphasizing what you already have. Work on increasing the Conversions to the people who are already in the store, increasing the number of items they purchase, and increasing how much they spend. That is where you will get your quick wins."

"I'm going to have to play around with some numbers later to see that for myself," said JJ as he wrote 'Lowest-Hanging Fruit First' in his notebook.

"Then once you've achieved a *10% Win* in each of the *7 Levers*, it's just a matter of continually *Cycling* through the levers to continue increasing profits," Charlie said, really emphasizing his pun this time.

JJ noted the last item in the process Charlie had written in his notebook—**Cycle**—as Charlie kept talking.

"You just need to make sure you schedule in time each week to be working on your *10% Wins*. Once you've Clarified each of your *7 Levers*, implementing a tactic to increase one will be surprisingly easy. It's just about consistency."

"Wow, thanks Charlie. Maybe I should start calling you 'coach,'" JJ grinned.

"I'll allow it." Charlie looked at his watch. "Glad I could help, JJ. But now it's time for me to head out. I need to get myself a better cup of coffee, and you need to start going after your *10% Wins*."

PRIOR PREPARATION PREVENTS
PISS-POOR PROFITS

YOU CAN'T LEVERAGE
WHAT YOU DON'T LABEL

YOU CAN'T MANAGE WHAT
YOU DON'T MEASURE

LOWEST-HANGING
FRUIT FIRST...

Chapter 6

Hitting the Road Running

Early the following week, JJ arrived at Cadence a few hours before opening. After talking to Charlie about the *7 Levers* process, he was eager to Clarify and Capture the *7 Levers* of Cadence. He decided it was better to do this when the shop was closed so he wouldn't be interrupted.

Inside the store, he turned on all the lights and dropped his bag in the storeroom. He sat down at the lunch table in the corner of the room and pulled out his notebook to get started.

He began by listing each of the *7 Levers* and then thought about how to Clarify, Capture, and Calculate them in the store. For a retail store like Cadence, JJ figured that his definition of Suspects would be the same as the one Charlie had used in the example of the shoe store: people who came into the store. That part was obvious, but how in the world was he ever going to measure each and every person who entered?

He couldn't really expect the team to manually count each and every Suspect like a prisoner marking off days on the wall of their cell. He remembered that when he was first opening the shop, he saw an ad in a retailer trade magazine for a machine that you could install by your door that would automatically count people as they entered. He made a note to buy one of those ASAP but realized he had no way of knowing his starting point. Measuring Suspects would therefore take at least a month after he installed the counter, so it wasn't a source of low-hanging fruit. He also thought about everything he'd already been doing to try and increase this lever, remembering what Charlie told him about how Correcting any problems in existing levers could result in some quick wins. Having previously believed that increasing foot traffic was the surest way to boost sales, he'd invested a lot of money into advertising and marketing, splurging on high-quality window signage, sponsoring a local race series, taking out ads in the local paper, and putting an ad in the Yellow Pages. JJ didn't think many people used the Yellow Pages anymore, but he thought it couldn't hurt. He made a note to cancel it after he started measuring Suspects to see if it made any difference to his traffic.

Realizing there was not much more he could do for now with the first lever, he moved on to Prospects. How could he differentiate casual visitors from serious buyers? It's not like people test rode the bikes before they bought them as they would a pair of shoes or a new car. He'd trained his staff to ask everyone who came to the store, "Can I help you?" but he knew this was a lazy way to go about things. How many times did people say, "No," and then go on to buy something? Most people who needed help asked for it anyway. He put a question mark next to Prospects and resolved to keep thinking about this one.

Conversions were much easier to Clarify and Calculate. All he had to do was see how many sales he was making each month. He opened his point of sales (POS) software and clicked on the reports section. He'd refrained from checking this as regularly as he knew he should have been because the numbers had been so dismal lately. Looking at it today, the knot that seemed to always be in his stomach tightened. So far he'd only made 134 unique transactions for the month. He winced a bit as he wrote the number in his notebook.

As he considered what he might do to bump these numbers up, he was mortified to admit to himself that he'd never actually trained his staff on how to sell effectively. They were athletes first, after all, not salespeople, but even after reading what seemed like dozens of books and articles on sales techniques, he'd never bothered to impart them to his staff. He recalled a quote he had heard years ago at a business conference: "What happens if you train your staff and they leave?" "Well, what happens if you don't train them and they stay?" He realized he needed to develop a specific process and set aside some time to train Matt, Dale, Emma, and Jess on it.

JJ was on a roll as he went back to his POS software to calculate his Average Item Price. This was a pretty easy lever to define. All he had to do was to divide his total monthly revenue by the number of individual items sold. He did the math quickly and wrote down the number in his book.

He knew that, in order to increase his Average Item Price, he would have to start selling more big-ticket items like bikes and race wheels, but how? He had put his more expensive and premium bikes in the front window to make them more prominent, and he often gave away a free helmet or cycling jersey with the more expensive bikes as a way to entice people to spend a little more. But the team had mostly pointed people to the sale bikes, like Dale had to Charlie, assuming they were doing them a favor by offering them the potential for a deal.

As part of his sales training, JJ resolved to encourage his staff to ask more questions of each customer to better determine what they were looking for rather than just default to the cheapest option. He knew that more serious racers would be willing to spend more on a better bike; they just might need some help determining which was best for them. "Helping customers is not about offering them the cheapest option," JJ muttered to himself. "It's about helping them find exactly what they need."

Items per Sale was another quick calculation. JJ referred back to the POS report that listed all the items sold and divided that number by the total number of unique transactions. He'd always been pretty good at upselling customers a helmet or light kit whenever they bought a bike, but he didn't think the rest of the team did this as frequently. The exception was Mike, who had always been diligent about suggesting additional repair and maintenance services like a degrease and wash to customers who came in for something else. He made a note to add this technique to his sales training.

Continuing down the list to Transactions per Customer, JJ realized he currently had no way to track this because he wasn't tracking individual customers in the system, even though the software allowed for it. This was a must-do for the team. He decided to have the team create a new record in the system for each customer that listed their names and mobile numbers so they could be searched for whenever they made a purchase.

The only thing JJ could think of when it came to his previous efforts to increase Transactions per Customer was the great customer service he tried to instill in the whole team. Of course, customers would return to stores where they had had a good experience, but even the best customer service relied on people deciding to come in only after they determined on their own that they needed one of your services. JJ needed a proactive way to remind people that it was time to come back to Cadence. He decided to sleep on that one for now as well and put a question mark next to that lever in his notebook.

As for increasing Margins, JJ would need to chat with his accountant to really figure this one out. He fired off an email straight away to ask for an appointment to review.

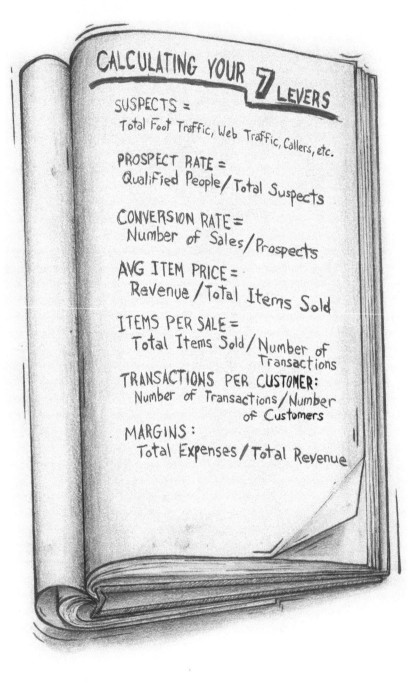

CALCULATING YOUR **7** LEVERS

SUSPECTS =
Total Foot Traffic, Web Traffic, Callers, etc.

PROSPECT RATE =
Qualified People / Total Suspects

CONVERSION RATE =
Number of Sales / Prospects

AVG ITEM PRICE =
Revenue / Total Items Sold

ITEMS PER SALE =
Total Items Sold / Number of Transactions

TRANSACTIONS PER CUSTOMER:
Number of Transactions / Number of Customers

MARGINS:
Total Expenses / Total Revenue

Satisfied with his work so far, JJ looked at his watch. He still had about half an hour before the shop opened, so he went online to search for a customer counter that he could install by the door to measure Suspects. He opened up the browser on his office computer, logged into Google, and typed "retail traffic counter" in the search box. At the top of the first results page was a link to www.RetailersRanch. com, an e-commerce site that appeared to specialize in tools and products for retailers. "Perfect," JJ said out loud to himself.

As he compared the different counters on offer, he noticed a model that could be hard-wired to connect back to your computer where it would download its data into a proprietary software package that you could export into other programs. As he went to click the big green add-to-cart button, JJ noticed an advert on the side of the screen for the same model but in a wireless version. This one was $100 more expensive than the other, and while he was hesitant to spend a single penny more than what was absolutely necessary, he also realized that he could potentially waste several days trying to install the wired version properly.

As he added the wireless counter to his shopping cart, he received a pop-up window offering a chime you could add to the counter that would alert you when Suspects entered the store. This wouldn't help him increase Suspects in any way, but it would, perhaps, make it easier for his sales team to notice new customers more quickly so they could approach them sooner.

"Hey, this is an automated way the store is increasing their Items per Sale," JJ said out loud as he added the chime to his cart. "Huh, let's see…"

JJ turned to the next blank page in his notebook and wrote, 'The 7 Levers of RetailersRanch,' at the top and began to jot down his experiences during this transaction.

Suspects: *Clicked on a Google ad, which is one way the store grows Web traffic.*

Prospects: *Started adding items to my cart, which signaled I was serious and prompted relevant internal ads to appear.*

When he got to Conversions, JJ realized he hadn't actually completed his transaction, so he pulled out his credit card. As he started to type in his payment and shipping information, he began to notice all the things the site had done to make ordering (converting) easy. The checkout form was free from distractions, had a prominent trust/secure logo, and featured a couple of testimonials from other customers, which made JJ feel confident in RetailersRanch. He also felt good seeing that the company offered free returns and exchanges, which brought JJ peace of mind since he could not afford a loss if the foot traffic counter turned out to be a waste of money.

By opting to buy the more expensive wireless model, it occurred to JJ that by the website suggesting he buy the wireless option, the company had figured out a strategy for increasing the Average Item Price by targeting customers with relevant but pricier items.

Plus, the pop-up suggesting the counter chime was a clear example of how an e-commerce site might increase Items per Sale, so JJ noted that in his book, too. A second later, JJ heard a little "ding" on his smart phone, indicating that he'd received a new email. He opened his inbox and noticed two new emails, one of which was a thank-you note from the store's owner, with a coupon code for 10 percent off his next purchase within thirty days. *What a great idea!* JJ thought, excited at having identified a tool that he could easily implement at Cadence. He knew these coupons were a great way to encourage repeat transactions. Sarah's nightstand was always stacked high with books she'd purchased from her local bookstore, which always printed a coupon on the back of the receipt.

He left the Margins section blank as there was no way for him to know what RetailersRanch.com's accounts looked like. He knew they benefitted from not having a physical location, but JJ needed the storefront. Having purchased several bikes throughout his athletic career, JJ knew that cyclists wanted to see their bikes in person before they bought one. He could relocate to a cheaper location, but the store's current position near the beach meant it was close to many of the most popular cycling routes in the area. He'd always felt this was worth the extra rent, though, short of moving the store, he had no way to know for sure. He resolved to think of other ways in which he could cut his Margins.

JJ checked his watch again and noticed it was time to open the store. As he left the storeroom to unlock the front door, he felt a little spring in his step at all he'd accomplished so early in the day.

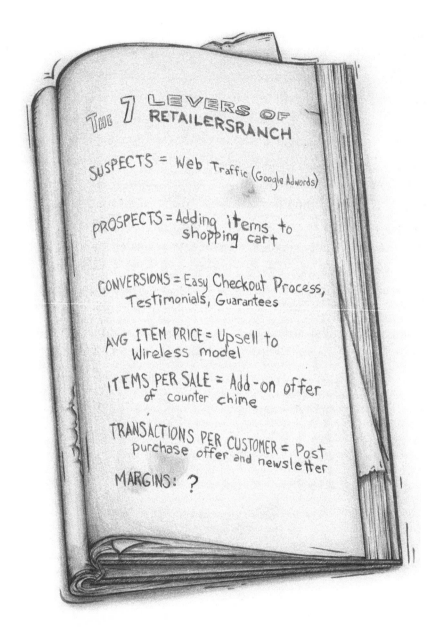

Chapter 7

A Friendly Competition

JJ checked his voicemail as he pulled into his usual parking space at the shop the next day. He had three new messages, including one from Dale. *Oh boy*, he thought. *What now?*

"Hey, boss," Dale's chipper voice said through the phone. "I pulled my hamstring pretty bad during a workout last night and won't be able to make it into work today. I should be good to go by the weekend though."

JJ groaned. He'd never expect one of his staff members to work through an injury, of course; He knew the damage that could cause. But he was annoyed that Dale hadn't even bothered to figure out a replacement for the day—and had waited until right before the shop opened to inform JJ he wouldn't be coming in. Once again, JJ felt like

Cadence was nothing more than afterthought for Dale. *He's probably just working here to get the employee discount on gear.*

JJ texted Emma, who, luckily, was free to cover for Dale. Given how slow business had been lately, JJ could probably have handled the sales floor on his own, but after Clarifying, Capturing, and Calculating the *7 Levers* of Cadence, he wanted to continue strategizing how he could generate some quick *10% Wins* at the store.

As he headed into the storeroom, he noticed the whiteboard he'd posted over his desk to keep track of everyone's hours in the shop.

Hmm. Maybe that could work, JJ thought as he stared at the whiteboard, an idea taking shape in his head.

He grabbed a dry-erase marker from his desk and drew a new chart on the whiteboard, listing the names of his staff and adding in columns for weekly and monthly sales per person. He had already figured out that in order to increase Conversions, he'd need to spend some time training his staff on sales techniques. He could certainly do this, but for now he would start by simply measuring the sales team by Average Item Price and Items per Sale. He made a column for each of those key performance indicators (KPIs) and listed all of the Cadence employees, including himself, to the side.

JJ wrote the new chart in large letters so the whole team could see it. He could have measured these levers privately if he'd wanted to, but he realized there was an advantage to letting everyone see how their coworkers were doing. They were all athletes, after all, and therefore had a natural competitive streak. Perhaps by seeing how their sales were doing compared to everyone else's, they might work harder just for the thrill of being number one. Maybe he could sweeten the deal by rewarding the top seller each month with some sort of bonus.

But first he had to get his team on board. JJ had always preferred to run a pretty loose ship and was hesitant about how his employees would interpret this new initiative. Charlie hadn't said so, but JJ was pretty sure having your salespeople resent you as a micromanager was not the best way to improve profits.

"Hey JJ. How's it going?" Emma had just arrived and popped into the storeroom to drop off her bag. "So Dale's out of commission, huh?"

"Seems like it," said JJ, happy to have Emma at the store today. At twenty-three years old, she was young and full of energy but was also extremely mature. In addition to working at Cadence full-time and running several marathons a year, she was putting herself through film school. JJ enjoyed listening to her talk about her favorite films and all the techniques she was learning. JJ had never quite let go of his inner teacher and thus loved seeing people around him get excited about school.

"What's that?" Emma asked, pointing to the whiteboard.

"Umm, well…it's our new sales initiative," JJ stammered. He'd thought he'd have more time to come up with an explanation.

"Cool! Tell me about it."

"Well, you know that guy Charlie who recently joined my training squad?"

"The one who's training for the IRONMAN?"

"That's him. He's also a pretty smart businessman and has been teaching me some of the techniques he uses to increase profits in his own companies. So, I'm just starting to implement them here. Basically, we're going to start tracking everyone's sales numbers and see if we can improve them over time. Don't worry, I'm going to give you some tips on how to do so. I thought displaying them on the whiteboard would give everyone an incentive to, you know, get their numbers up."

"Ah, so it's a competition, huh?" Emma folded her arms and looked serious for a minute. "You know, Jess is going to hate this."

"Oh, really? Why?" JJ asked, getting nervous.

A wide grin spread across Emma's face. "Because I'm going to kick her butt!"

JJ laughed. He knew Emma and Jess were good friends. A little one-on-one competition might actually be fun for them. "I'm glad you're enthusiastic, but let's keep it civil, shall we?"

"No problem, boss," Emma said as she headed back out to the sales floor. "Seriously, though, I think it's a fantastic idea!"

* * * * *

JJ need not have worried about how his sales staff would react to the whiteboard idea. Over the next couple of days, Jess and Emma became newly motivated by their numbers and, with no additional training from JJ, started posting some small gains for the store, mostly by suggesting that customers buy additional items to complement their purchases. Combined, their Items per Sale had already increased by 6% while their Average Item Price was up 4%. Even JJ had started becoming more effective.

But not everyone was as enthusiastic.

"Sup, boss?" Dale called loudly as he sauntered into the storeroom at 8 a.m. on Saturday. This was his first day back at work since his injury, and JJ had taken the opportunity to schedule his first sales training session with the whole team before the store opened at ten.

Before JJ could respond, Dale noticed the whiteboard on the wall. "What's this?" he asked. His eyes scanned the chart and landed in a dead-stop at the weekly sales figures for the other team members. Emma was in the lead.

"Hey, buddy, how you feeling?" JJ asked, looking up from the paperwork to which he'd been attending. "Is the hamstring better?"

"What?" Dale turned and looked at JJ, his eyes glazed over. "Oh, yeah, yeah. Much better. When did you put this up?" He pointed to the whiteboard.

"While you were out," JJ said. "I got the idea from Charlie, my IRONMAN trainee. I've been trying to figure out how to boost sales, and he said measuring was a good place to start. The whiteboard turns it into something of a game. Jess and Emma have been having a lot of fun with it, actually. And, as you can see, their sales are higher than they've ever been before."

Dale was silent for a moment. "I don't know if I like having my business splashed all over the board for everyone to see. What if I'm having an off-week? Like *this* week, for example."

JJ was growing irritated with Dale's lack of initiative. "Everyone else is on board with it, champ, so you're gonna have to participate, too. Look at it this way, if sales go up, your commissions go up, too. And a little friendly competition can go a long way. You're used to having your cycling times posted whenever you compete, right? Same thing."

"Whatever," Dale mumbled as he put his bag away.

In that moment, Emma, Jess, and Matt entered the storeroom. "This better be good," Jess joked. "Saturday is my day off, you know."

"I know, Jess, and I don't plan to keep you here long today, but now that Dale is feeling better…" he stole a quick glance at Dale who was frowning in the corner. "I wanted to go over some sales techniques to help you boost your numbers even more. I realize I never properly trained you on these, which was a mistake and a missed opportunity—not only for the store, but for each of you, since these tips are sure to increase your commissions."

"Sounds good to me," Emma said.

"And Matt, I realize you're not on the sales floor, but these techniques can also help you increase the number of services you can provide to customers who come in for repairs. I imagine you'd like to be a bit busier than you have been."

"You got that right," Matt said. "Don't get me wrong, it's been great to catch up on my podcasts, but I imagine that's not why you pay me the big bucks."

In contrast to Dale's bad attitude, JJ noticed the easy banter and casual joking that came so naturally to him, Jess, Emma, and Matt. Dale could be charismatic, but he never really fit in with the rest of the group. For the first time, it occurred to JJ that Dale might not have a place within the new Cadence. He hated the thought of firing one of his employees, but if Dale didn't show significant improvement, he might not have a choice.

For the next two hours, JJ practiced various techniques with the team.

"Don't think of it as selling a bunch of stuff to people just so you can boost your numbers," JJ advised as he explained the concept of increasing Items per Sale. "Think about it as helping people get everything they need rather than waiting for them to tell you what they need. They might not know how big a difference the right set of wheels will make for long-distance rides or the importance of knowing your watts or cadence by using a bike computer. Have a conversation with them. Ask them about their goals and use it as an opportunity to showcase other products in the store that they might be able to use. It's a win-win-win scenario: you get some more sales under your belt; the store profits; and the customer walks away with everything they truly need."

"What we need to do right now is open the store," Emma said. "I've gotta try out these ideas while they're still fresh in my mind so I can keep beating Jess!"

"Just you wait until I've had a good night's sleep, Em," Jess teased. "Remember, I know more about cycling than you do!"

"Alright, ladies," JJ laughed. "We're done here for now anyway. Emma, go ahead and open the store. Jess, go home and take a nap!"

Chapter 8

The Prospect of a Win

The following Friday, JJ was at his desk going over the numbers and updating the whiteboard. Earlier in the week, he'd told Charlie about his new initiatives and couldn't wait to see how they paid off so he could share the numbers at their next training session. To his delight, the whiteboard competition and the sales training was already making a difference. The Average Item Price was up from around $500 to $535—a 7% increase—while Items per Sale were already up 10%, from 1.1 to 1.2.

Emma and Jess had really started to master the techniques he had taught them. The other day, he'd watched Jess outfit one customer with a new set of race wheels, a helmet, gloves, a Cadence jersey and bike shorts, and even a new water bottle. "It's got a special type of insulation that keeps the water colder for longer. I use it myself," she'd said. JJ couldn't help but be impressed at how easy she made it look.

Even Matt had used the techniques to his advantage, suggesting that he tune up a customer's gears when he came in to replace his tires: "It's only twenty dollars extra, and regular adjustments like this can really extend the life of your bike."

Unfortunately, Dale had not fared so well. His numbers had actually gone *down* after the training, which JJ found baffling considering how long he usually talked to customers. Clearly Dale was so caught up in talking about the sport—and likely boasting about his latest results—he barely thought about selling, even to prime Prospects like competitive cyclists who, JJ knew from experience, were always looking for some new gear or gadget that could improve their performance. *He's a good kid*, JJ thought. *But he doesn't get it.*

Just as JJ was considering Dale's future at Cadence, the young triathlete entered the room. "Boss, can I speak with you before you leave tonight?" Dale asked with a lot more bravado than JJ would have expected given his poor performance this week.

"We can chat now," JJ replied. He had a feeling he knew what was coming next.

"With the new season approaching, I need to upgrade some of my gear," Dale said. "The race wheels I've been riding are as old as this shop, and they're just not up-to-scratch these days."

JJ nodded and waited for him to go on.

"How about sponsoring me some more this season?" Dale continued, warming to his pitch. "My race times are getting stronger, and I'll no doubt be on the podium a lot more in the local series this season. It'll be great exposure for the shop."

JJ paused for a moment before he responded. JJ loved sponsoring employees. It was one of the dreams he'd had when starting the store—helping kids fulfill their aspirations through sponsorship and great deals. And it was the thing he missed most about teaching, really helping the next generation. But he was simply in no position to help Dale out this year, especially considering that Dale didn't seem the least bit interested in returning the favor.

"Listen, Dale, you know I'm a huge believer in your ability and pumped to see you doubling down on your training, but the business can't afford it right now. I'm more than happy for you to buy any gear you want at our wholesale pricing."

He hated saying no to Dale, not just because he wanted to help the kid out, but also because it reminded him of how Cadence wasn't fulfilling his own dreams. Even with the improvements he'd seen in the past week, he was still a long way from being where he wanted to be. The thought made him a little sick to his stomach.

"What about asking Jules from ProSport to help out?" Dale said, not skipping a beat and breaking JJ's internal monologue. Clearly, he had anticipated JJ's pushback and rehearsed this counterpoint. "They sponsor a bunch of athletes, and your friendship with her has to count for something, right?"

Where is this sales tenacity on a daily basis? JJ wondered. If only he was this persistent with customers, the store would probably be in a position to support him with those race wheels.

"All I can do is ask," JJ said, knowing full well that Jules would never agree to sponsor Dale until JJ got current on his account. But he didn't want to admit that to Dale.

"Thanks, boss, you're the best. See if you can push her for the new triple-milling aluminum set they launched."

* * * * *

JJ was in the storeroom the following Thursday, changing into his training gear, when he heard the chime sound from the new customer counter he'd installed the week before. "Hello, is anybody home?" a voice called out from the front of the store.

Oh no, JJ thought. He'd completely forgotten that this was the day Jules was due to visit, and he wasn't ready yet money-wise. "Be right there, Jules!" he answered as he adjusted his shoes and picked up his training bag. Trust Jules to pop in during the last fifteen minutes of the day.

"So who's guarding the fort?" Jules teased as JJ came back into the retail area, dressed for a full training session.

"You caught me on my way to the track to meet my training squad." JJ smiled lightheartedly hoping to hide his nervousness. Despite their easy friendship, he felt a knot form in his stomach because he knew what this visit was about: his extra thirty-day grace period with ProSport had just expired and he hadn't settled his bill. It was ridiculous to think ProSport wouldn't notice, but he hadn't had the nerve to call up and ask for more time.

"Oh, I won't keep you long," Jules said, flipping her long blonde ponytail behind one shoulder. "By the way, did you hear about Zach Wallace's win on the weekend?"

Zach was an old friend of both JJ and Jules from the competitive cycling circuit. Eleven years earlier, he'd landed a contract with a pro-cycling team and, just the weekend before, had won a classic one-day cycling race in France in a little over six hours. JJ and Jules had lost all contact with Zach after he moved to Europe with his team, but the news of his phenomenal win brought back good memories of their younger years and the friendships forged during that time.

"I'm still in shock," said JJ, shaking his head. "That has to be the toughest one-dayer of the season. Also, didn't he fracture the radius bone in his right arm two months ago? How could he possibly have trained while he was recovering?"

"Oh, you didn't hear how he pulled it off?" Jules said.

"Guess not."

"He spent those months training in his garage on a computer simulator," Jules said. "You know the one that was released about six months ago?"

"Oh, right!" JJ had heard about these simulators. Part training tool, part multiplayer online game, they were rapidly transforming the typically boring indoor training session into an enjoyable and realistic experience, allowing cyclists of all ages and abilities to sync their bikes, trainers, and computers up with one another and ride against other people in the virtual world. As you rode, your computer would sync with your bike's speed sensor and power meter as you biked up virtual mountains. It would even increase resistance on your pedals in order to make the training as realistic as possible. JJ could see how this would especially benefit someone who had been injured, as it would work the muscle without the bumps of the road getting in the way of the healing process.

Thinking about the simulator, JJ thought back to Charlie's example of the shoe store putting in a treadmill to allow customers to test shoes out before they bought them. Charlie had mentioned that this tactic had increased sales significantly. Suddenly, JJ had a brilliant idea.

"That's it!" he screamed. He was so excited, he almost kissed Jules.

He would set up a simulator in the store and encourage customers to "try on" a bike right there in the shop. Hooking a bike up to the simulator would only take a minute and would also turn the buying experience into something fun that no other store in town was doing. It would also be a great way to identify Prospects because who wouldn't want to go for a test ride before spending $2,000 or more on a bike? He might even be able to convince a few customers to buy a simulator so they could train at home if they were injured or the weather was bad.

"Wait, what?" Jules said, laughing at JJ's outburst. "What did I say?"

"I've been trying to think of a way to push more sales," JJ stammered in his excitement. "And adding a trainer like Zach's would be a great way to turn Suspects into Prospects by having them self-select to try it out!"

Jules raised her eyebrows. "Hmm, not sure I got all that. But if it will increase sales, I like it. In fact," Jules paused and JJ could see the wheels turning in her head. "I may be able to get ProSport to give you one of our trainers to use as part of a joint promotion."

"That'd be awesome." JJ grinned. He knew instinctively that this new tactic would bring positive energy into the shop and was a great start towards another *10% Win*.

Jules and JJ chatted amiably for a few more minutes before Jules's tone suddenly turned serious.

"You know I don't like to pressure you, JJ, but I have to keep my boss off my back. When we spoke last, you said you would be able to make your account current within the extra thirty-day period, but we haven't heard from you. Can you bring your account current by the end of this week?"

JJ felt the knot in his gut grow tighter. "One more week. Just give me a week and I swear I'll settle it."

"That's what you told me a month ago," Jules said, her voice kind but stern. "Are you sure this time? 'Cause there is no way I can get you that simulator if you're not current, and my boss won't allow me to extend your account much longer."

"Yes, I promise. I've just been going through a slow patch lately, but business is picking up," he lied.

An awkward silence filled the space between them, and JJ could sense Jules's doubt. But having done all she could, Jules picked up her briefcase and turned for the door. "One week," she said, glancing back. "One week, JJ."

As soon as she was gone, he flipped over the "closed" sign and locked the front door. He couldn't escape the shop fast enough.

Chapter 9

Widening the Margin

The following week, JJ called up ProSport and settled his account using the company credit card. He knew it wasn't a long-term solution, but he needed to buy himself time—and hopefully get that simulator. Luckily, it was enough—for now at least—and Jules agreed to ship him one overnight.

"I owe you one, Jules," JJ said, grinning nervously into the phone and barely containing his relief.

"Don't sweat it, JJ. It's a really cool idea, and you're the first client of ours who's suggested it. If it works, it could be awesome for us." *Of course*, JJ thought, *this is as much an opportunity for them as it is for me.* Now it just had to work.

"Can I assure Dave we'll be back on a sixty-day basis from here on out?"

He was a beat too slow in replying. "Sure," JJ said, hoping his old friend wouldn't press him any more on the topic.

"Great! Talk to ya' soon, JJ."

As JJ hung up the phone, he felt a gust of warm air from the beach blow in the front door as Charlie walked in, dressed for a run.

"Hey, coach, question," he said as he approached the counter. "I'm five weeks in, so why am I only seeing 10 km training runs in my schedule?" As he finished his question, Charlie dropped his keys in a tray behind the counter. Like a lot of JJ's athletes, he'd arranged to leave his car keys at Cadence while he went for a 10k run on the beach. After his run, they planned to grab a cup of coffee and discuss Charlie's program for the coming weeks. "The IRONMAN is a 42k race. Shouldn't I be learning to run that far?"

"Nice to see you, too," JJ shot back good-naturedly. He had known it was only a matter of time before Charlie asked him this question. All his athletes did at some point. "What time do you want to run your IRONMAN marathon in?"

"I'm hoping around four hours," Charlie said.

"Great. So a four-hour marathon is a five-minute, forty-two-second-kilometer pace," responded JJ clearly having done the math before. "So you won't run a four-hour marathon, until you can comfortably run a fifty-seven-minute 10k. In fact, you'd want to be running a sub-forty-five-minute 10k, as fatigue and everything else kicks in on race day. Once your 10k pace is solid, then we increase it to 15k, get that foundation in place, then 20k and so forth," JJ added. "As they say, you can't run until you learn how to walk."

"Oh, you mean the old incremental-gains approach, right? After my run, remind me to tell you a story about that from a business perspective. By the way, how're things going here at the shop? Sounds like you and your team have been making significant strides. Get it...strides?" Charlie said, miming a runner's pose.

JJ paused before answering. He and his team had been making progress, but after his call with Jules, it didn't seem like nearly enough to matter. "It's going okay. We've put some KPIs in place for the sales crew, which seems to be working well. Most have embraced it, and we're getting results there. I also talked to one of our account reps, Jules from ProSport, who agreed to loan us a virtual-reality-type simulator that we can hook up to our bikes so customers can give them a test run before they buy. I thought it would be a great way to turn more Suspects into Prospects—kind of like the treadmill idea."

"I like it!" Charlie said. "Sounds like fun, too."

"Yeah," JJ said, trailing off slightly.

Charlie noticed the change in JJ's demeanor. "What's the matter? You don't seem all that happy."

"It's just that all of these *10% Wins* ideas are great, and I can see them starting to work, but I'm still behind on my accounts and I don't know what to do. Before you came in, I had to settle one of my accounts using a credit card, which buys me a little time, but I need a more long-term solution."

"Fair enough. What about your Margins lever? Have you done a little audit of your expenses, like my accountant's son did?"

"Ah, well, no," JJ replied sheepishly. "I do have a catch-up with my accountant scheduled, but I haven't had it yet."

"Mate, you don't need to sit down with your accountant to get a Margin *Win*," Charlie said. "There are tons of ways you can start reducing overheads and saving cash. All you have to do is start by looking at all your expenses. Then you can see what expenses you have that are just a waste. I'm sure there are services, software, and other things you've been spending money on that you can eliminate pretty easily. And for ones you can't get rid of entirely, call each supplier and see if you can get a better deal. I'd bet you $500 you're still on plans that are obsolete, or that your suppliers offer new packages and pricing that didn't exist when you first opened your account. But they're not going to proactively offer you a lower price; you need to call and ask. You could save a bundle in just a few minutes."

"Sure thing," JJ said, feeling a little better now that he had some sort of a plan of action. "I'll do it first thing Friday when one of my other employees are in the store and I have a morning free. But what about suppliers like ProSport? I can't just cancel them, and I'd bet you $600 they won't give me a discount given the state my account has been in with them lately."

"I'll take that bet," Charlie said confidently. "You could get a nice win with them by negotiating a target rebate program."

"Target rebate? How does that work?" JJ had never heard of this before.

"Let me guess—you're paying the same rate today that you did when you opened, right?"

"Yes, that's right."

"So you're probably still on their basic partner pricing," Charlie said. "This basic level represents the least-valued and smallest customers a supplier has, and it's where they typically start all new accounts. But it's standard practice for suppliers to have various pricing tiers—bronze, silver, gold, etc.—as customers grow, expand, and start to sell more of the supplier's product."

"Ah, okay, volume discounts. That sounds great, but as you can see, my numbers are still pretty low and haven't really grown since my first quarter with them."

"Sure, your volume is low today, but you've just told me things are growing, and as you cycle through the *7 Levers*, things will continue to increase exponentially. So, here's what you do. Call your account rep—you know her well, right?—and negotiate that if you hit one of their higher sales tiers—silver or gold level, or whatever they call it—before the end of the summer season, they will retroactively apply that discounted buying rate to your orders all season and give you a rebate. The difference between bronze and silver could be as high as 8%, while the difference between silver and gold could be another 5% savings, so you're looking at some pretty high potential margin reductions—and another *10% Win*—if you can pull this off."

"I wonder why Jules never mentioned this before," JJ said. "Is this common business knowledge and somehow I didn't get the memo?"

"Everything's negotiable—you just need the right people in your corner," Charlie said with a wink. "Besides, it's a win-win. It's a target for you to hit, which is no doubt one of your rep's own performance goals since she has to try to grow the Cadence account for ProSport. Plus, it's also a limited risk for them because if you don't hit the targets, they don't owe you anything. You're not putting them in a bad position by asking for a discount when your account is not in great shape."

"I'll definitely try to negotiate the target-rebate deal," JJ promised.

"Great," Charlie said. "Well, I'm off. See you in a bit, coach!" And with that, Charlie sprinted out the door.

Chapter 10

Getting Back on Track

"**G**ood run?" JJ asked as Charlie came back into the store a little over an hour later, his face noticeably redder than it had been when he left.

"Yeah, there's nothing like running on the beach," Charlie said, sliding onto a stool next to the checkout counter. He chugged from his water bottle and swiped the back of his hand across his mouth. "Ready for that caramel macchiato?"

"Speak for yourself," JJ said with a wry grin. "I like a manlier drink."

Thirty minutes later, they found a table on the terrace of the local coffee house and sipped steaming hot beverages.

"So you're clocking your 10k at just under an hour, right?" JJ asked.

"Yup. Today I was at 57 minutes."

"Great. You'll definitely be able to get to marathon pacing in the time we have left."

"Thanks, coach." Charlie smiled, clearly pleased with the progress he was making. "So what about your progress? Earlier, you seemed a little underwhelmed with where things stand at Cadence."

"Yeah. Like I said, I can see this *10% Win* thing working long term, but it just isn't fast enough right now. Don't get me wrong, I think the target-rebate program idea is genius, but I can't wait until the end of summer to save cash. I need ten times the customers, not a 10% increase. Sure, sales have been up, but it's still not enough. I've got a mortgage, and school fees for two kids not far away."

"A ten-times increase?" Charlie queried rhetorically. "Tell me how's that worked out for you in the past?"

JJ had tried a lot of things over the years. It wasn't that he was lazy. He put as much determination into the store as he had with his own triathlon training. He thought back to the chubby adolescent he'd been, and how, with persistent effort, he'd transformed his body. He had put just as much energy into his teaching at school, and then his business—except this time it felt like the effort wasn't paying off.

"You see, it's all about incremental gains," Charlie said. "You can't cook in a Michelin Star restaurant until you learn how to dice onions properly. You can't run before you can walk, as you pointed out to me earlier. And, you can't make a million dollars before you know how to make $10,000. In fact, I don't know how to make a million dollars, nor does any millionaire I know! If you want to become rich, you must give up the idea of making a million."

That got JJ's attention because he knew Charlie was easily worth a few million dollars.

Noting JJ's look of exasperation, Charlie continued slowly. "You see, 'making a million dollars' is very different from 'making millions of dollars.'"

"The media loves to tell us stories about the savvy—usually young—entrepreneurs who made millions or billions of dollars in a flash by selling their hot new ventures to the highest bidder or managing a successful IPO. These stories are so popular that they seem almost common, and might lead you to think that the best way to make a lot of money is to have a brilliant idea that you cash out on quickly."

"But throughout the history of business, most millionaires have become wealthy over *time* not overnight. Think about the celebrated American industrialists. Rockefeller, Ford, Getty—they didn't get rich by cashing in on a one-time idea. They started small, building their companies dollar by dollar over the course of decades. Their wealth wasn't lightning in a bottle; it was the result of hard work and intelligent, consistent strategy, which meant it was repeatable and sustainable."

"I'd hardly consider myself a Rockefeller," JJ said.

"Just because you're not an oil tycoon doesn't mean you can't learn something from the man," Charlie said, patiently. "This is the exact logic I followed when I was growing my own businesses. Sure, the idea of becoming the next Mark Zuckerberg and being able to retire as one of the wealthiest men in the world before the age of thirty was appealing, but how many people have become rich this way? Perhaps a couple of dozen? Thousands, if not millions, of people have become millionaires by doing things the old-fashioned way. Including myself.

Charlie paused while he stirred his macchiato.

"It took me about five years of deliberate and consistent effort to have a net worth of over a million dollars. Even now, though I'm worth a few million dollars more, I'm only adding to my wealth in

$100,000 increments, not million-dollar ones," he continued. "Sure, one day, if we take a business public, I might actually make a million dollars in one single transaction, but that's a *big* if.

"When business owners tell me that they are only interested in making millions, what they are really saying is that they are not interested in the reality of entrepreneurship. They want to deceive themselves with highly improbable fantasies about becoming rich and famous. The truth is this: It takes a lot of tenacity and focus to become a successful entrepreneur, no matter how you define success. If you want to become rich in business, you must give up the idea of becoming a millionaire. You must start from where you are today, and gradually learn to generate sums of money *one digit at a time.*"

JJ looked a little deflated and confused as Charlie shifted to another one of his stories.

"Look, when I started out making money, I was in my teens. I was a referee at our local basketball association earning about $7 a game. Then when I went to college, I started working at the shoe store I mentioned to you when we first met. There I learned a lot and earned about $12 an hour—an extra digit more than I'd been earning before.

"After university, I was lucky enough to land a job at a company that consulted on marketing and growth to other businesses. My boss was brilliant, and I got exposure to tons of different industries. But I was still an employee earning about $20 an hour. I worked hard, studied everything I could, and after implementing what I had learned, I was able to get a regular monthly bonus. This enabled me to grow as an employee and budding entrepreneur, and those bonuses were able to increase my wealth by a few hundred dollars at a time— *another digit.*

"A couple of years after I started that job, I realized that I would have to do things differently to increase my wealth by more than $100 at a time. So I got serious about becoming wealthy and started my own side business selling sports memorabilia. The product that business sold was around $500, and, as you know from experience, starting your first business is a huge learning curve. That little side hustle helped continue my growth as an entrepreneur, and I was able to put around a $1,000 *per week* into my pocket after expenses. A significant increase, but still not millions.

"So I had learned to increase my wealth-building from single digits blowing a whistle as a teenager, to four digits by creating and selling a product."

JJ couldn't help but be impressed. He thought of his years as a teacher—doing something he loved but settling for a limited income. His foray into the retail shop, and the coaching business, served as tangible reminders that he wanted to attain a certain level of wealth, too, one that would provide more security and opportunity for his family.

"You've barely touched your latte, coach," Charlie said, glancing down at JJ's rapidly cooling beverage.

JJ followed his gaze and laughed, having forgotten all about his coffee while listening to Charlie's story. "What can I say? Your story got me hooked." He lifted his mug to take a sip. "Go on."

Charlie took up his narrative again. "I then took the profits from that little side business and started a real company with some business partners. After a few years of long hours, hard work, and an education in hard-knocks, that business began to grow and we were able to make profits in the tens of thousands each month, meaning I'd learned how to get rich $10,000 at a time—*another digit.*

"Since then, I've become a serial entrepreneur, and have spent the last ten years or so learning, growing, and building out other projects and companies with staff. The teams in these businesses now produce revenue in the multimillions, and the profits have made me a millionaire. But here's the thing, when you really look at it, those companies only really earn revenue by makings tons of little sales for hundreds or thousands of dollars. And my personal wealth is just built in increments of $100,000 dividends—*another digit*. So I can't say that my knowledge of getting rich has gone beyond earning $100,000 at a time."

JJ shook his head. "Still, you gotta admit, earning $100,000 dividends is more than most people earn in a year. Your past learning curve is my present goal."

"But do you know what?" Charlie said, leaning forward, his eyes wide. "After years of entrepreneurial education and effort, I've learned how to build sustainable wealth, and that's all I can ever ask for. And it's all anyone should ever ask for. You have to learn each step in the sequence: first get richer by $100, then $1,000, then $10,000, then $100,000, and then maybe one day $1 million increments. Do you have your notebook with you?"

"Always," JJ said as he pulled the notebook and a pen out of his bag and handed it to Charlie.

"It generally goes something like this," Charlie said as he opened to a blank page and started writing.

"You first earn single-digit wealth as a casual employee. Then you grow to double-digital wealth as a full-time employee. After you become more valuable to your employer, you can start earning triple-digit wealth in bonuses or commissions, or by maybe taking the leap to be self-employed.

"As you take those skills and begin to transition toward being an entrepreneur and generating profits via your own product, you learn to put thousands of dollars into your bank account at a time. That's four-digit wealth.

"Then as you continue to progress, begin to employ staff, and leverage yourself, you're typically earning five-digit wealth and can consider yourself a skilled business owner. Six-digit wealth comes as you grow into a true entrepreneur and learn how to bank $100,000 dividends or profits." He spun the notebook around so JJ could see what he'd written.

JJ smiled at the irony. "Like first running a fifty-minute 10k, then building to a four-hour marathon."

"Touché," Charlie said. "And that is what the *7 Levers* philosophy is also built on. Achievable incremental growth, continued *10% Wins*, each and every time, that add up to incremental and sustainable bottom-line profit growth."

"Thanks for putting that in perspective," JJ said. "I want that type of growth, not the flash-in-the-pan overnight millionaire kind that can be erased in an instant. I guess I'll just keep cycling through those levers until I get up to speed."

"Or think of it this way," Charlie said, as he downed the last sip of his macchiato and stood up to leave, "You named the store Cadence after the cycling term, right?"

"Yeah," JJ said. "It's another term for your pedaling rate."

"Right, so to get faster and win races—and to succeed as an entrepreneur—you need to Cycle through the levers and just increase your *cadence*."

GETTING WEALTHY ONE DIGIT AT A TIME

$7 per hour = Single-Digit Wealth →
Casual Employee

$25 per hour = Double-Digit Wealth →
Full-time Employee

$100 bonuses = Triple-Digit Wealth →
Commissioned Employee or Self-Employed

$1,000 profits = Four-Digit Wealth →
Product Owner (Entrepreneur journey Begins)

$10,000 profits = Five-Digit Wealth →
Business Owner (with staff leverage)

$100,000 dividends = Six-Digit Wealth →
True Entrepreneur

$1,000,000 increments =
Seven-Digit Wealth → IPO
or Sale of the Business

Chapter 11

Searching for Suspects

"I meant to tell you. I called Jules at ProSport and ran your idea about the rebate past her." JJ and Charlie had peeled off from the usual Tuesday night squad session around the track when JJ decided to fill his business mentor in on how things were faring at the shop.

"Oh yeah?" Charlie was trying to conserve his breath and decided to let his coach do most of the talking today.

"Yeah. She told me if I get to the silver level by the end of the summer, she'll give me a rebate—just like you suggested."

"That's great," Charlie panted.

"It is, though I still don't know how I'm going to pull that off. I installed the simulator a few weeks ago and it's definitely working. I'm now able to track Prospects more efficiently and they've definitely increased since we started using the simulator. Bike sales are already up over the weekly average, and the whiteboard experiment between my sales staff is helping boost Conversions and Items per Sale. We're up about 7% each on those, but I just don't know how I'm going to sustain this growth unless I get more customers in the store. I need more traffic!" JJ could feel himself getting worked up despite all the endorphins coursing through his veins thanks to the vigorous run.

"Right. Suspects," Charlie said. "I was wondering when you'd start asking about that. Every business owner always wants to know how they can increase their traffic."

"Do you blame them?" JJ was starting to get indignant. "Traffic and Suspects are the most important thing for a business!"

"Of course they're important," Charlie conceded. "But, remember, they're just one of the 7 *Levers*. Tell you what. Let's continue this conversation after our session today. I'm too winded to talk much right now."

JJ looked over at Charlie who was bright red and dripping sweat. He laughed. "Haha. Fair point. This is your coaching session, not mine. Which reminds me…we need to pick up the pace!" JJ sped off ahead of Charlie, encouraging him to catch up to the rest of the squad.

* * * * *

After the run, Charlie and JJ found a picnic table in the park near the track where they could catch their breath. There was a mild breeze coming off the water and the sun was just starting to lower itself toward the horizon.

"Tell me," Charlie started after taking a long slug from his water bottle. "Before you met me, what type of marketing did you do to attract new customers or suspects?"

"I tried a little bit of everything," JJ said. "I tried some online and social advertising, including a Google AdWords campaign. I also took out a few ads in a couple of cycling and triathlete magazines, but those turned out to be a waste of money since most of their readership doesn't live in Bayside, and they're not going to make a special trip to buy a bike."

"You've got that right," Charlie said. "And what tactic ended up being the most successful?"

"The Google AdWords campaign by far."

"Do you know why it was so successful?" Charlie was clearly a fan of the Socratic method.

"Because it's targeted. I could design the campaign so that ads only showed to people within a twenty-mile radius. Plus the ads only appeared if people searched for terms like "bike store" or "where to buy a bike," so they were already on the market to buy."

"Ding ding!" Charlie said. "So often business owners make the mistake of trying to market to the greatest number of people possible, thinking that the more exposure they get, the more successful they'll be. That's true to a point, but getting that type of exposure requires so much money, time, and effort that it's never the most efficient way to boost sales."

"Yeah, I thought having an ad in one of the premier cycling magazines would be good for our brand," JJ said. "But it ended up being a waste of money—and it cost far more than the Google campaign."

"I'm not surprised to hear that," Charlie continued. "I like to think of marketing as a hierarchy. There are some potential Suspects who are better targets than others because some people are simply more likely to buy from you than others. And once you know who those customers are, it's pretty easy to find them. Who is your ideal customer?"

"Someone who lives in the area and is in the market for a bike or bike accessories," JJ said.

"Right. They have a problem or a need and they're looking to solve it. Now, if you were one of these customers, how would you go about solving your problem of needing a new bike?"

"I'd go to Google and search for where to buy new bikes in my area," JJ was starting to wonder where this was going. He knew all of this.

"I know this may seem obvious since you've already had success with Google AdWords," Charlie said, as if reading JJ's mind. "But I'm trying to make a larger point. It's not about the tool you use to advertise or market your business; it's about knowing which customers you're trying to reach and using the tools that best suit those customers. Google AdWords worked for you because those who are looking to buy a new bike like the ones you sell are usually pretty young and therefore use the internet to search. I'm a big fan of Google AdWords and use it with a lot of my clients, but not all of them. In fact, a few years ago, I worked with a company that offered in-home nursing care and physical therapy for seniors. Since older people aren't as tech savvy, I told the company to take out an ad in the Yellow Pages instead of relying solely on Google. They thought I was crazy—who uses the Yellow Pages anymore? The answer—older people, and many of their potential clients when looking to solve their problems."

"So basically you want to start with the lowest-hanging fruit again—the people who are already searching for your services and are therefore easy to market to?" JJ asked, making the connection back to the *7 Levers*.

"Exactly! And once you've captured the lowest-hanging fruit, you can turn your attention to the slightly more difficult to reach Suspects. In your case, this might be someone who has been toying with the idea of buying a new bike or taking up cycling but isn't actively searching for one. However, if they came across an ad for a bike store, they might decide to take action. To reach these people, you might try a social campaign that advertises to people near you who have expressed an interest in cycling online."

"But isn't social advertising a good way to reach people who are actively looking for a bike as well?" JJ asked. "The reach on social is so much greater than it is for search-based marketing."

"It's true that the reach is bigger. But if you needed a new air conditioner installed, would you really search for that on a social network? Or are you there to find out what your friends had for breakfast and are doing next weekend?"

"Good point," said JJ. "I'm on socials to see photos and updates from friends across the globe. If I needed a new air conditioner, I would search Google." Even as he answered, the light bulb went off.

Charlie nodded. "If someone saw your ad on Facebook and ended up buying something, they would have been in that category I just described—they may have been thinking about buying a new bike but weren't actively searching for one. I call these people 'procrastinators'. They are one level higher than the lowest-hanging fruit, whom I call 'searchers'."

"Nice," said JJ. "So I can still do the Facebook campaign, but focus on my Google campaign first?"

"Spot on," said Charlie. "The cost and responsiveness of the Google leads will be much better for your bottom line. So you should start there."

"Got it, I'll work on getting a *10% Win* and increasing my Suspects through Google—and next time I'm working on that lever, I'll do the Facebook ads."

"Not so fast there, cowboy. Don't move on to marketing to procrastinators until you have milked the searchers dry. You haven't maxed out that level until you can say your marketing is standing right there in front of *all* the searchers when they start looking. So, if someone knows they need a new bike, where else might they go in addition to Google to search for one?" asked Charlie.

"Ah, well, there are a few websites and portals specifically for bike sales which we can advertise on," JJ said.

Charlie smiled. "Well done, kemosabe. Every industry has a range of places and avenues people go to when trying to solve a problem. You just need to make sure you get in front of those hungry crowds first, before you waste time and energy on a higher level in the hierarchy."

"Levers, levels," replied JJ. "Maybe you should get some new names that aren't so similar. But first, can you tell me more about this marketing hierarchy?"

"That's a story for another time, mate," Charlie said. "Right now, I've got to go home and eat dinner. I am starving after the workout you just put me through."

Chapter 12

Perception vs. Reality

"I can't just increase our prices by 10% like your accountant did," JJ said, setting his coffee cup down with a louder thump than he intended. "Sure, the bikes we sell are great, but a number of other stores in town stock the same brands, so we have to be competitive."

JJ and Charlie were back at Jerry's Diner to catch up early on a Saturday morning, and the conversation had naturally turned from IRONMAN training to the *7 Levers*.

"I'm not asking you to *just* increase your prices by 10%," Charlie said. "What else can you offer along with the purchase that adds perceived or real value that doesn't cost you anything? Identify that and you'll know what to do."

"Perceived value? What's that?" JJ asked.

Charlie paused to think of an example. "We're going out for dinner in a few weeks, right?"

"Right," JJ said.

"Well, what's the difference between where we are going and, say, this diner here?" Charlie asked.

"Well, the other place charges three or four times more for a meal," JJ joked, knowing all too well he'd be paying for the meal like he always did at these pre-race celebration dinners.

"Exactly. And why is that? Essentially a meal is a meal, and I do love the omelets here."

"Well," JJ started. "The place we're going is definitely fancier than this. They offer free ciabatta, the dining room is nicely decorated, and they have this fantastic sommelier whom you will love."

"I'm sure I will. But what about the meal? Is their spaghetti Bolognese much better than the pasta you can get here?"

"Umm, come to think of it, probably not," JJ laughed.

"Exactly. So they charge a lot more because of the *perceived value*—all the extra things they offer with the meal: a nicer atmosphere, wine experts, delicious free bread, etc. Your bikes are the exact same pieces of aluminum and carbon-fiber that the guy down the road sells, so the only way to justify selling them at a higher price is to add some sort of additional value to the purchase. What can you offer customers, beyond the bike itself, that they would be willing to pay a premium for?"

JJ ran his hand through his dark brown hair, which was just starting to turn silver at his temples. "Maybe I'll take this one to my team, let them brainstorm ideas with me."

"Good idea," Charlie said. "You'd be surprised how many ideas a group can generate in a short period of time."

As JJ left the diner, he texted his team: *Can you all stay late on Monday for a staff meeting? I'll bring pizza.*

* * * * *

On Monday morning, JJ was in his office reviewing last week's numbers. As usual, Dale was dead last in sales and had shown absolutely no improvement since the whiteboard competition had started several weeks prior. At this point, JJ was actually losing money to keep Dale around and the time had come to make a hard decision: he was going to have to fire Dale.

Later that day, just after Dale's shift but before the staff meeting, JJ summoned Dale to his office.

After some very forced small talk, JJ cut to the chase. "Look, Dale, I know you aren't happy about the new sales initiatives we've started around here, but I need to keep my business running, and I can't afford to have anyone on staff who isn't going to work as hard as everyone else. You're a good kid—and a fantastic athlete—but sales is just not right for you. So…I'm going to have to let you go."

Dale was silent for a moment, during which he looked like he might try to defend himself. But, perhaps realizing JJ's decision was final, he stopped. "Sorry I let you down, boss. I thought I was doing okay, but once I saw the numbers, I saw how far behind I was. I guess I was so focused on training that I didn't think about it."

"Well, look at it this way, champ," JJ said trying to lighten the mood. "Now you can use all that extra time to train even harder. You're so close to being able to go all in. If you focus right, the pros are not that far out of reach for you. I know it!"

"Thanks," Dale said, halfheartedly. He got up to leave, looking crestfallen, but JJ knew he'd get over it soon enough. As Dale sauntered out the door to the storeroom, the rest of the team came in, looking a little confused.

"Where's Dale going? I thought this was an all-staff meeting," Matt asked.

"I'm afraid I had to let Dale go just now," JJ said. "I hated having to do it but, as I'm sure you've noticed since we started tracking everyone's sales, he just hasn't been performing as well as the rest of you."

"Yeah, we know, boss," Emma said sympathetically. "It sucks, but we understand."

"I bet you did him a favor," Jess offered. "He's more interested in his training anyway. Now he can devote his full attention to turning pro. In the long run, it'll be a win-win."

"I like that attitude, Jess," JJ said. "And, for what it's worth, you guys are doing a great job. Last week we posted $5,000 more in sales than the week before."

"Woot-woot, way to go, Emma!" Matt called, pumping his fist in the air.

Emma blushed but couldn't keep from smiling. "Stop it, you guys."

"Yeah, great job, Em," JJ added. "Those two big-ticket bike sales you got put us over the top."

"You'd better watch your back, though," Jess teased. "I'm nipping at your heels and plan to overtake you in sales next week."

Everyone laughed and bantered for a few minutes, then JJ cleared his throat. "Okay, here's the deal: I need your help. You've heard me talk about the *7 Levers* I've learned from my triathlete trainee, Charlie. Well, the biggest thing we've gotta nail down is how to increase prices by 10% across the board. Of course, we can't just jack up the prices on our merchandise since that will drive people to our competitors, so we have to figure out a way to add some sort of other value that we can include with the cost of our bigger-ticket items. I'm, frankly, a bit stumped by this, but it occurred to me I've got a goldmine in brain power right here with our team."

"Don't flatter me, boss!" Emma joked, feigning embarrassment at the compliment.

"Wouldn't dream of it, Em," JJ said. "Okay, so, I got pizza like I promised—extra anchovies for everyone! Just kidding. Grab a plate and a slice, and let's get started."

The team dived into the pizzas and gathered around the table where they usually ate lunch.

"I've got some time on my hands," Matt said as he bit into a slice of pepperoni, ready to offer the first idea of the brainstorm session.

JJ nodded. "Go on."

With that encouragement, Matt warmed to his subject. "Why not give away a free bike service or two with every sale. It won't really cost anything to deliver the service, as you're already paying my wage whether there's something to do or not."

The reminder that he was paying Matt to provide services no one seemed to want felt like a knife in JJ's side, but he couldn't deny Matt's idea was a really good one. Bike services usually cost customers $50–$100, so giving away two services with every sale would help justify the increase in prices, keep Matt busy, and not really cost JJ anything extra.

Matt continued. "Plus, getting people back in the store for their free service might mean they'd buy something else while they're here. You never know. Also, I know of a bike store in Boulder, Colorado that has a bunch of videos on their website teaching people how to change a flat tire and stuff."

He paused to swallow a mouthful of pizza. "Why don't we record some of these ourselves, but instead of giving them away on YouTube, we only give access to clients when they buy a bike. It will show clients we really care about them because it will save them some time and money in the long run."

Emma lifted her hand, like the student she was. "I'm studying film this semester at college, so I could easily borrow a camera and some lights from school."

"Hey, why not record some of your training squad sessions on bike handling and riding technique?" interjected Jess. "It would take the tire-changing stuff to the next level."

"I like it," JJ said, happy to see everyone chipping in and so enthusiastic about helping to grow the business.

"Why not even allow people to come along to one of your squad's bike sessions?" Jess said, adding to her idea. "You charge your athletes to do those group sessions, so it's worth something, and it might even lead to them joining the squad."

The meeting ended in laughter and a ledger full of good ideas JJ was ready to implement. As he bid farewell to Jess, Matt, and Emma, JJ bit into the last slice of pizza and smiled.

Chapter 13

Drafting Off the Team

Just as JJ finished filling up his water bottle in the shop, his cell phone rang. It was Charlie.

"Hey coach, I'm really sore from the run yesterday. My right calf is super tight. Do you think it's a good idea to ride today?

"Absolutely not!" JJ responded immediately. "You don't want to waste a training session on junk miles. IRONMAN training is all about quality over quantity, so rest up. You don't want to make it even worse and injure yourself."

"Thanks for the advice, coach. I'll do that. But, hey, weren't we supposed to chat about your *7 Levers* again after our session? I want to hear how the price increase strategies your team suggested have been working out."

"Yeah, but it can wait," JJ said, though he couldn't help but be disappointed.

"Tell you what," Charlie said. "I run a monthly advisory call with some of my clients who also use the *7 Levers*, and we happen to have our next one tonight at eight. I can still do it while I'm resting my legs. Why don't you sit in on it and see if you can get something out of it?"

"So, a mastermind group?" JJ asked, having been involved in one a few years back without much success.

"Heck no," Charlie replied, sounding a little offended. "These are structured board meetings with an agenda and accountability. They started out as regular check-ins with the marketing managers of our various projects to make sure they were on track and to ensure they were regularly working on a business lever. We'd have all our projects rolling through the *7 Levers* at the same time, one lever every month. Each manager would focus their team for an entire four-week period on getting a *10% Win* in that lever.

"What we found, though, was that the day-to-day running of the businesses often got in the way of executing a long-term strategy. Distractions happen; it's business. So we started these regular sessions with everyone. We'd get together for about ninety minutes, and I'd start the session by redefining the lever we were focusing on for the next four weeks—Suspects, Items per Sale, Margins, whatever. I'd often share stories I'd found of other businesses getting *10% Wins*, and then we'd focus on each project or business unit one by one. Finally, everyone would discuss, share, and create an action list for getting their projects or division, a new *10% Win* that month. There was no hiding, total accountability, and even a little rivalry built between the various managers. One of them even coined the name 'Advisory Board.' I started to invite a few other business owners I knew to these sessions, and it's evolved into its own thing now."

"Count me in!" JJ said, his disappointment fading as quickly as it had appeared.

* * * * *

At 7:55 p.m., just after he put Ben and Emily to bed, JJ sat down at his laptop in his makeshift home office and logged into the online meeting room Charlie had arranged for him. As the time on his laptop hit 8:00 p.m., his screen came to life. Suddenly he heard Charlie's voice through his speakers.

"Hey everyone, Charlie here. If I sound a little more alive this week than I have recently, it's because I hurt myself training yesterday and my coach gave me the day off. So I'm a fraction more rested than usual. That's about all I'll say on that this week, as JJ, my coach, is actually joining us today. Are you there, coach?"

Not realizing he'd be asked to respond so early, or in fact at all, JJ fumbled with his headset microphone and got out a muffled "Yep."

"Great," Charlie replied. "As most of you know by now, JJ owns a great bike store here in town called Cadence. While he's been helping me prepare for this IRONMAN I'm doing in a couple of months, I've been helping him with the store and applying the *7 Levers*. I wanted to invite him along today as we discuss this week's Advisory Board session topic, Items per Sale.

"Now, as always, before we dive in, let's keep you accountable and do a quick check-in. The last Advisory Board session was focused on Conversions. So what did you guys implement and what were the wins?" Charlie asked. "Dave, do you want to kick things off?"

"Sure thing, Charlie," replied a voice whom JJ could only assume was Dave.

"Last time we worked on Conversions, we focused on increasing the Conversions of the sales team on the phone, but this round was all about *online* Conversions, so we started by split-testing the checkout pages of our shopping cart," Dave began. "We tested the layout of the order form page. We also tested whether adding some more secure shopping and trust icons to the webpage would help, and whether adding a testimonial on the checkout page would boost Conversions. It only took the development team about two days to get everything in place, and then we let the test run for the month and pulled the results yesterday."

"Well, come on, get to it," Charlie said in a half-joking way.

"It looks like the layout change wasn't a good one, as that reduced Conversions. But the security and social elements got us a really nice bump of 4% combined."

"Niiiiice," Charlie responded. "Jen, you're up."

"As most of you might recall, I spent the month completely redoing the proposal I use when quoting on my design jobs," a woman's voice said. "Rather than sending the details in the body of an email like I was, I've created a six-page proposal that I can quickly customize for each client. It's got samples of my previous work, testimonials from a couple of regular clients, awards I've won, and an area where I can insert the job scope and pricing. So far the new form has worked a treat. I've converted 50% of the business I've quoted for so far this month!"

"That's incredible!" gushed Charlie. "Now, just to manage *your* expectations, it might not stay at 50%, but even if it washes out to, say, a 40% Conversion rate, that's a massive increase from where you were before. Something like a 24% *Win*, right?"

This type of accountability went on for the next ten minutes as the other six people shared their actions and wins since the last session: 8%, 11%, 9%, 9.3%, 14%, and 6.2%.

"Alrighty then," said Charlie. "Let's get into the core of today's Advisory Board. Let me kick off the discussion with a story."

Everybody groaned in unison. "Oh, knock it off. You know you love my stories."

After a few laughs, the group grew silent and let Charlie continue.

"This morning, I went to Bayside Sports Massage to get my calf looked at. As I left the studio, I ended up walking out with a bag of what looked like dirt. It was magnesium to put in my post-training baths."

"That stuff's a miracle-worker," JJ interjected.

"I hope so," Charlie continued. "Anyway, I don't know if the massage therapist offers magnesium to every client, but the waiting room has a shelf covered in everything from extra-large elastic bands and bags of this dirt, to balls of various shapes and sizes, and a huge collection of supplements. This was a perfect example of an effort to increase Items per Sale, the topic of today's session."

As the Advisory Board session turned toward the main discussion, the various business owners talked about their projects, how they each defined Items per Sale, and what they were doing currently. The group discussed ideas, examples, and tactics for improving this lever.

For the online and e-commerce retailers among the group, it was things like offering cross-sells on their websites' thank-you pages or "Often Purchased With" packages like the ones JJ remembered seeing on Amazon.

Jen, the graphic designer, who was clearly new to the group, decided to offer a letterhead and business card design as a package with her logo work. She would make it easy for clients to select this option by listing it in the proposal she mentioned earlier in the board meeting.

For Greg, the owner of a swimming pool business, someone suggested he team up with his brother-in-law and offer paving around the outside of the pools as part of the initial sale. It was something his customers pretty much always arranged themselves separately anyway, so why not offer it as an add-on and treat it as an additional Item per Sale he would get a commission for? Greg liked the idea so much, he left the Advisory Board meeting to call his brother-in-law right away.

"What about you, JJ?" Charlie asked, catching JJ off guard. "What are some ways you could increase Items per Sale at Cadence?"

"Well, uh, to be honest, I wasn't planning to speak up tonight so I haven't given much thought to it."

"Then why don't you tell the rest of the Advisory Board about the store and see if they have any ideas?"

JJ proceeded to tell the board members about the history of Cadence, the problems he'd been having, and the ways in which the *7 Levers* had started to help his business. "I haven't cycled through everything yet, though," JJ explained. "So I have yet to strategize on Items per Sale beyond simply training my team on some upselling techniques."

"I have a suggestion that might help." This came from Tim, a guy who ran a pest-control business on the other side of the globe.

"We have our Ant-Eaters—that's what we call our team—go into a client's home with a clipboard and checklist," Tim said. "They go through the entire home, checking everything for everything. It makes these guys look professional and thorough. From there, we advise the client on what services are best suited for them based off the checklist. Clients really respond well to this. It implies so much, especially that we really care about our clients and have a standardized system in place, which they can see us put into action.

"When we first implemented this across the business, we kind of dropped the ball and didn't really teach the guys how to communicate or use the checklist in front of customers," Tim continued. "We just started making them use it, and that alone saw our services per client jump from around 1.2 to 1.6—an incredible 30% increase.

"After I got my big ass kicked at a board meeting for not training the team, and we actually invested in teaching them some basic presentation skills—how to do the dance so to speak—our Items per Sale rose dramatically to the current rate of about 2.5. So maybe you can do something like that at Cadence," Tim suggested. "Create a checklist of what a wannabe pro cyclist would need when buying a bike. You do sell doping kits, too, right?" he laughed.

"That's a really good idea, Tim. I'd never thought that selling bug spray could help sell bikes," JJ said.

"A good idea can come from anywhere," Charlie said. "That's one of the other perks of these calls."

"Yeah, I could create a checklist for triathletes, road racers, parents buying for their kids…" JJ's mind started racing, causing the rest of the Advisory Board meeting to become a blur.

* * * * *

After the call ended, JJ was feeling newly invigorated and immediately opened up a blank document on his computer to start working on his checklist. He was so engaged, he lost track of time and almost didn't notice when Sarah walked into the room.

"Hey sweetheart, come to bed. It's almost eleven," she said, her voice immediately soothing to JJ despite his high energy.

"Oh wow! I lost track of time. Thanks babe," he said as he closed his laptop and followed Sarah into the bedroom.

"What were you up to in there?" she asked. "I thought I'd lost you for a while."

"You know that guy Charlie I told you about? The one I'm training for his first IRONMAN in a few weeks and who's been helping me with some ideas for Cadence?" Sarah nodded. "Well, he invited me to this really helpful group call where I got a great idea for the store."

"That's great, sweetie," Sarah said, yawning. JJ knew she was interested in the store, but it was late so he'd tell her more about it some other time. "Hey, aren't we supposed to meet Charlie and his wife for dinner in a couple of weeks?"

"Yeah. I'll probably get us a reservation at Delano's. You like that place, right?" JJ already knew the answer.

"Ooh! Yes! That's my favorite." Sarah paused and her face fell. "Too bad I don't have anything nice to wear."

"What about that dress I bought you for our anniversary last year? I thought you liked it, but, come to think of it, I don't think I've seen you wear it. I guess I haven't taken you out that much since then, huh?" Now it was JJ's face that fell.

"Oh, no! It's not that," Sarah said, looking a little sheepish now. "It's just that, well, I love that dress, and I've actually taken it out a few times to wear it. But I realized after you gave it to me that I don't have any shoes that match, and I couldn't justify splurging on a new pair given the financial stress we're under."

That stung JJ a bit. "I wish you would have said something. You know, I actually wanted to buy you a pair of shoes to match at the time, but I didn't trust myself to pick out the right kind."

"Well, the salesperson should have been able to help you with that," Sarah said. And then a thought occurred to JJ. If that sales assistant had offered to sell him a matching pair of shoes to complete the outfit—trying to increase her own Items per Sale and get a *10% Win*—they all would have benefited. Sarah would have had a complete new outfit, JJ could have been proud to take her out in a dress he chose, and the clothing store would have bagged an extra sale.

Of course! JJ thought. *Sales isn't about giving customers what they know they want, it's about ensuring my customers have everything they need.* It was his job to create a store environment—from the way the merchandise was arranged to how the salespeople interacted with customers—that made it easier for customers to walk away with everything they needed—not just what they came in the door for. The checklist idea would certainly help with that, but rearranging the items in the store could also work wonders.

That would be a project for tomorrow, though. Tonight he was happy to have a few quiet moments with Sarah. He kissed her lightly and took her in his arms as they fell asleep side by side.

* * * * *

Over the next few days, JJ worked on remerchandising the store to help boost Items per Sale. He couldn't believe it had never occurred to him to put bike tubes and chain lubricant right next to the cash register as a bit of point-of-sale marketing. He also placed an order for some energy bars, which he hadn't before stocked, knowing that a lot of his customers came in right before or after a ride and that some quick food-for-fuel might make a good impulse purchase. These weren't big ticket items but, he thought, *incremental gains*.

The following weekend, he met up with Charlie again at Jerry's to discuss Charlie's training and digest the takeaways from the Advisory Board call. JJ had been working diligently on executing the checklist idea and was excited to show Charlie the result.

"It's pretty basic right now," JJ said as he slid a few pieces of paper over to Charlie. "But once I get the content down, I thought I'd work these up into some well-designed brochures—maybe even hire Jen from the Advisory Board to design them for me? Unlike with Tim's business, it doesn't really make sense to have my sales team go over a full checklist with a customer; it might look tacky and unprofessional. But if we turn them into a buying guide and hand them out to customers when we first approach them, they can get ideas for what they might need to buy on their own—things they might not have thought about otherwise."

"That's a fabulous idea!" Charlie said. "You're really catching on. By inviting people who would otherwise be window-shoppers or tire-kickers to look at these buying guides, not only will the Cadence team increase Items per Sale, but as a byproduct they would turn more Suspects into Prospects, plus give the sales team some structure to their conversations, thus increasing Conversions as well."

Charlie could see the lights going on in JJ's eyes—a sign that the *7 Levers* were taking root and becoming second nature to him.

"Let me ask you something," JJ said.

"Sure," Charlie replied.

"Some of the people on the Advisory Board seemed to have taken massive actions, while others made relatively small changes. What do you make of that? I mean, creating a bunch of checklists is a lot of work, which I am happy to do, but running split-tests like Dave said he did on his website seems pretty easy."

"Well, it's all relative," said Charlie. "Every business or Advisory Board member is at a different stage, selling different products or services, in a different market. A lever that it is easy for one person may be difficult for someone else. You can't compare your effort to theirs—it's not fair on yourself. Think of it this way, I've had to work a heck of a lot harder than others to improve my cycling times, yet I've come a long way in the pool time trails with far less effort."

JJ nodded in agreement to that last analogy as Charlie continued.

"And remember, some of the people in that Advisory Board have done this before; this might be their third or fourth time through the levers. They've done some heavy lifting already, maybe in previous cycles, maybe in other levers. It's not about big wins one month and then stagnant growth the next. It's about consistent *10% Wins* each month. It's about your business *cadence* if you will," Charlie said, grinning at his pun.

"You say consistent *10% Wins*," JJ countered, "but on the call, people were reporting 4% *Wins*, 16% *Wins*. It wasn't really consistent."

The waitress brought their omelets and refilled their coffee cups.

"Thanks Anna," Charlie said before he responded to JJ. They had been coming to Jerry's so frequently that they were on a first-name basis with the staff.

"Very true, and a very good point," Charlie said after Anna left. "I try to look at it from an entire *7 Levers* perspective. During any cycle, some levers are going to outperform others. You might find a new traffic source does really well and provides 15% more Suspects, while you can only increase your Conversion rate by 8%. Perhaps you try two different ways to increase your Transactions per Customer at one time—one gets a 4% jump and the other a 6% jump, combining to a *10% Win* there.

"But when you step back and look at your business after you've worked through all *7 Levers*, you hope that it all balances out and provides the bottom line result you want. As much as I may say things like 'get your *10% Win*,' the true goal in all this is to have a clear, consistent framework in which you focus on improving one of the *7 Levers* at any given time so you can achieve steady *10% Wins* and, thus, a steady doubling of profit, without getting caught up by vanity metrics or what the other guy is doing. It's about knowing your business and doing what works for you."

"That makes sense. I'm already noticing a lot of variance in my numbers. Since I started cycling through the levers, my Conversion rate is up by 8%, but my Items per Sale is up something like 16%. I'm sure that will go up again when we start distributing buying guides, though it will probably even out over time."

"Exactly. Which is why you keep cycling and strategizing." Charlie was almost finished his omelet by this point. "Man, I was hungry. Ever since I started training, I feel like I could eat a horse three times a day."

JJ laughed. "I know, which is why I'm taking you out for Italian food as your celebratory dinner. The place we're going has enormous plates of pasta."

"Can't wait," Charlie said.

Chapter 14

Can I Interest You in Some More?

D elano's Trattoria was always packed on Saturday nights, but
JJ had made a reservation.

"Ah yes, table for four," the maître d' said. "Your table
is ready. Is the rest of your party here?"

"We're here!" JJ and Sarah turned around from the host's desk to
see Charlie and a beautiful young woman enter the restaurant.

"Just in time, champ," JJ said. "Charlie, this is my wife, Sarah.
Sarah this is Charlie."

"I've heard a lot about you," Sarah said. "You might be helping
my husband out more than he's helping you!"

"I don't know about that," Charlie said as he reached out to shake Sarah's hand. "It's a pleasure to meet you. This is Chloe."

"Great to meet you, Chloe," JJ said, extending his hand. "I promise to have your husband back to you in about a month."

"Eh, it's nice to have the house to myself once in a while," Chloe said teasingly. "I get to watch whatever I want on TV. It's lovely to meet you, JJ. Charlie can't stop gushing about how well you've trained him."

"It's true," Charlie said, punching JJ lightly on the shoulder. "This man here is a miracle-worker."

"So you're a triathlete widow too, huh?" Sarah said to Chloe. "You have my sympathies."

"Right this way, ladies and gentlemen," the maître d' said, leading the two couples to a courtyard lit up with fairy lights in the foliage.

As the waiter sat them at their table, JJ noticed a bottle of wine in the middle of the table. The bottle had a small swing tag around it that read "Welcome to our restaurant. Tonight our Sommelier Antonio Doubé has recommended this bottle from the Montepulciano d'Abruzzo region. It pairs perfectly with the specials we have prepared. We hope you choose to enjoy it with your meal."

"Items per Sale," JJ said to Charlie, pointing to the bottle. He signaled for the waiter to open it for them and pour glasses all around.

"Haha, you're learning," responded Charlie.

"It's amazing how much I keep doing this, and how often the idea of *10% Wins* just pops into my head," JJ said as Sarah groaned good-naturedly.

"Don't get him started," she deadpanned.

"It's true," JJ continued. "I keep seeing *10% Wins* everywhere. It's really something."

Charlie laughed. "That's awesome. Means it's becoming second-nature. Just what you want."

Deliberately shifting the conversation, JJ said, "So how're you feeling about the race? Do you feel ready? Have I whipped you into shape hard enough, champ?"

"If it gets any harder than this, I'm a dead man," Charlie quipped. "Though Chloe's pretty pleased at the six-pack that's starting to show."

"'Starting' being the operative word," Chloe winked at Charlie. Clearly, JJ noticed, they had a chemistry on par with that of him and Sarah.

"Seriously, it's been great," Charlie said. "I couldn't have asked for a better trainer. I just hope I do you proud on race day."

As the wives began to talk among themselves, JJ and Charlie's conversation drifted back to the bike store as it so often seemed to do.

"I've been thinking about the Transactions per Customer lever a lot lately, and I'm just not sure what to do," said JJ. "Sarah and I chose the location of the store because it's close to the main road for the exposure to passing traffic. That's been great for new business, I think, but it's not like we're in a shopping mall where we can get lots of foot traffic and customers can just easily wander in again and again."

Charlie waited for JJ to continue, not wanting to interrupt his flow.

"I did try one thing to get more MAMILs into the store," JJ said.

"MAMILs?" Chloe asked.

"Sorry," JJ said. "It stands for 'Middle-Aged Men in Lycra.' It's a silly term we use in the sport to describe the non-professional riders. Anyway, I tried to attract more MAMILs to meet for their group rides at the store every weekend by putting a bike pump and big Gatorade tub at the entrance. That way the riders can fill their drink bottles for free at the store and pump their tires before they set off. It seems to be working; more riding groups are meeting at the store, and the same riders are there each week, but none of them have their credit cards and they're not really interested in buying anything. So I guess it's increased repeat traffic to the store, but not really repeat transactions."

Just as Charlie was about to respond, Chloe piped up. "Wow! This wine is amazing!" She reached across the table to take a look at the label on the bottle. "Oh, I've heard of this. I read about it in the Garagiste newsletter!"

"Chloe works in wine distribution and is a bit of an oenophile," Charlie said, turning to JJ.

"What was that name you mentioned?" JJ asked Chloe. "Garage sites?"

"Garagiste," Chloe corrected. "It's the only email-based wine business in the world. It was started back in the '90s by this guy Jon Rimmerman who got the name from a French winemaking movement. It's kind of amazing actually. He only built a website in 2010. Before that, you had to hear about his business—which was really just an email list—through a friend. Then you had to request to join by emailing them directly. It was sort of like those fancy speakeasy bars that are so popular nowadays. You know, the ones that have no sign on the door and you need a password to get in? And yet, despite the fact that they don't work that hard to attract customers, they pull in tens of millions of dollars in revenue every year. Everyone I know in the industry subscribes."

"How do they actually sell wine?" JJ asked, intrigued by this seemingly effortless business model.

"Rimmerman roams the world, looking for small producers making flat-out fantastic wine, stuff usually not found outside the region," Chloe explained, clearly excited at the opportunity to talk about her industry. "Then he sends an email blast to his subscribers that talks about his terrific finds. If you're interested in a bottle or two, you reply to express your interest and get sent an invoice. Once you pay, you can pick the wine up at their warehouse outside of Seattle or have it shipped to you. But they only ship twice a year when the weather is best for wine transport."

"Wow," JJ said.

"I know," Charlie said. "When Chloe first told me about this site, I was extremely impressed."

"So what makes his emails so great?" Sarah asked.

"They're so much fun to read!" Chloe exclaimed. "They aren't some stuffy sales pitch. Each one tells a vibrant short story that you can't help but get lost in. Rimmerman really tries to transport you to the places where he travels."

"I'm glad you're paying attention," Charlie said to JJ.

"Me? Why?" JJ asked.

"Because Chloe just gave you a great idea to help increase your Transactions per Customer."

JJ was confused. What did wine have to do with a bike store? Cadence barely had a website! He waited for Charlie to answer.

"Email," Charlie said with emphasis.

"Email?" JJ hated that he sounded like a parrot.

Charlie continued. "Just get the email address of all your customers when they buy. Then, based on the type of bike they buy—triathlon, road racing, commuter, kids, mountain bike, etc.—send them a series of emails over a three- or four-month period with tips, suggestions, and other product recommendations. It's all about regularly reaching out to your past clients, keeping them engaged with your business, and they will think of you when they are ready to buy again."

JJ nodded, taking this all in. "That sounds like a lot of time and emails each week."

"If you were to send each email individually, sure. But you can do it once and automate it. Just like the buyer's guide checklists you've created, sit down and create a series of six or seven emails to match each type of buyer. When you're getting the Transactions per Customer lever in place, you can then set up a system that will automatically send those emails out. So all you need to do is ask your clients for their email address so you can send them some tips and advice to get the most out of their new bike, and then add them to the relevant email list. It's like having a little sales person on auto-pilot reaching out to your past customers and giving them a friendly reminder to come back."

"That's all well and good, but I'm no Hemingway," JJ declared. "My grammar and spelling are terrible. Plus our website is barely functional, and I can't afford to add an online store."

"Jon Rimmerman leaves typos and grammatical errors in his emails on purpose," Chloe said, making JJ think she and Charlie made a stellar team. "It helps them come across as more authentic."

"There you go," Charlie added. "And who said anything about e-commerce? In your emails, just tell your customers to call you with their credit card details to order what you recommend—just like Jon does. You don't even have to force your clients to come back into the store. Remember, it's repeat *transactions*, not repeat *traffic* we want."

"Well, let's toast to that!" JJ said, raising his glass and clinking it against the others. After that, JJ felt himself relax into the conversation. He could have blamed it on the wine, but he suspected it was something else entirely.

Chapter 15

Keeping Your Eyes on the Road

JJ paced Charlie as he took laps in the swimming pool of the aquatic center. After ten more laps, both men collapsed against the side of the pool to recover and catch their breath.

"You're ready, champ," JJ said as they headed into the whirlpool to rest their muscles. "Just two more weeks to showtime!"

Charlie nodded and toweled his hair dry. "Unbelievable. Hardly seems it's here. The training has made these past five months fly by." He gave JJ one of his signature grins. "How 'bout you, coach? Is the bike business *rolling* along?"

"I've been going at those *7 Levers* like a guerilla," JJ said, laughing. "Got bit by the bug, you could say. In addition to all of the things we've talked about, I've bought a ton of new books, set up a bunch of new social media accounts for the store, subscribed to some cool marketing lists, started a podcast, and joined several online groups to learn even more about business and marketing. I've…"

"Slow down, slow down," Charlie said, as JJ was talking a mile a minute. "I applaud the enthusiasm, but let's start from the start. You mentioned setting up a bunch of social media accounts. Tell me about that."

"Well, I was sitting with Scotty, my brother-in-law, a few weeks back at a family barbecue, and we got to talking," JJ began more calmly. "He was showing me this new social media tool that apparently everyone is using, and he said that we need to get Cadence an account and start posting photos and videos to it. He thinks it will generate a lot of exposure for the store."

"Sounds interesting," Charlie responded in a tone JJ couldn't read. "Go on. You mentioned something about a podcast as well?"

"Yeah well, I've subscribed to a bunch of podcasts—everything from business to bicycles—and thought we could make a really cool show that combines triathlete interviews and tips for the coaching business with stuff from the bike store. I could easily get some great guests on the show, and I'm sure Jules and other suppliers would be able to make their sponsored athletes available for interviews as well. I was listening to another podcast about how easy it is to create a podcast, so I ordered a computer media kit a couple of weeks ago, and we've already recorded three episodes," JJ said, clearly proud of all that he'd accomplished.

"Let's put the brakes on a little here. It's sounding like you're spinning at too high a gear," Charlie said using another silly cycling metaphor.

"What?" JJ was surprised to hear Charlie's reaction. "I thought you'd be proud of the initiative I'm taking."

"This is a common pitfall I see in a lot of business owners, especially once they start executing the *7 Levers*. They get so excited about doing different things that they start to confuse *action* with *achievement* and *tactics* with *strategy*."

JJ paused to reflect on the conversation he'd had with Charlie at the beginning of their twenty weeks together. Could he really have gotten off track?

"So tell me *why* the social media again?" Charlie asked.

"Well, a lot of people use social media, and the podcasts I'm listening to talk about these various platforms all the time," JJ said. "I don't want to be late to the party or miss out on an opportunity to attract new business."

"Sure. And your own podcast, how's that going to help the business?"

"Well, as I said, I'm really enjoying the podcasts I'm listening to. I'm learning tons, and I'm sure our own podcast would give a lot of new exposure to the business. Plus I'd get to connect with some cool athletes and other coaches. But come to think of it," JJ said as something occurred to him, "Charlie, you don't have a big social media following do you?"

"As the great philosopher Kenny Powers once said, 'I play real sports. I ain't tryin' to be the best at exercising.'" Charlie said, trying to keep overt sarcasm out of his voice. "Can you pay your account to Jules in downloads, followers, or exposure?"

"Well, no," JJ said a little sheepishly. "But all those things will lead to profits."

The timer on the whirlpool buzzed, so the two men climbed out to shower off the chlorine. They met back up fifteen minutes later in the aquatic center's atrium for a smoothie.

The thread of business conversation picked up where it had been dropped. Charlie grabbed a pen from his gym bag and began to write something on the back of his training plan.

"Show me how," he said as he spun the piece of paper around, showing a list of the *7 Levers*, with a big "= PROFITS" at the bottom. "Just like all businesses, your profits are made up of the *7 Levers*, correct?"

JJ nodded.

"So show me, as you said, where social media fits among the *7 Levers* and leads to profits?"

"What do you mean?" JJ said, realizing he was in for another valuable lesson he had to pay attention to.

"Well, you said 'all those things will lead to profits,' so for that to happen using, say, social media, it has to increase one or more of these *7 Levers* in a clear and effective way—and be the best way to increase that lever right now. Otherwise, it's a waste of your focus. So show me how using this particular social media tool will increase profits."

"Okay, well, umm…" JJ stammered.

"Let me ask you this," Charlie said as he watched JJ struggle to answer him. "How can it help you increase your Margins? Will your suppliers give you cheaper prices because you have thousands of followers? Can you pay your staff or landlord less because a post got shared a bunch?"

"Ah, not really, I guess," JJ said as Charlie put a big line through the word "Margins." "What about increasing Transactions per Customer?"

JJ instantly had a good answer here. "Well, if we regularly post updates and photos, it will keep the store front-of-mind for our customers, and that will lead to them coming back in more often."

"Sure, that's a reasonable and often-used argument," Charlie said, giving JJ a little confidence. "However, what percentage of your actual customer base do you think you can convince, easily, to connect and follow you on that particular platform?" He raised his eyebrows.

"Probably a pretty small fraction," JJ conceded. "And only a fraction of those will actually end up being repeat customers."

"Exactly," Charlie said. "What about increasing your average Items per Sale? You can't 'sell' access to your social media profile as an additional item. So it can't help you here either," Charlie said, not waiting for a reply from JJ. "Same goes with increasing your Average Item Price."

"Hang on," interrupted JJ. "What about preeminence? If we demonstrate social proof that we are the leading bike shop in town, with the most followers and the best content, can't that help justify a higher price in store?"

"That's a fair point," Charlie said with a twisted grin, acknowledging his protégé's determination and thought process. "It's not the best argument, but it does have some merit. Sure, perceptions can equate to reality, so being known as the most popular store in town can help, but it's a stretch. It doesn't necessarily mean a customer will pay more for something they can get elsewhere for less.

"Now, until you have an online store, or enough followers, you can't really sell directly via any social posts, so increasing Conversions is out of the question," Charlie continued.

"And I guess, given that Suspects only become Prospects when they are in the store and show real intent to purchase something, the Prospect lever doesn't fit either," chimed in JJ as he began to understand where Charlie was going with this.

"Exactly," Charlie said.

"But Suspects…it could be great for those, right?" JJ continued. "We could reach a whole new range of Suspects who don't know much about us right now."

"Kinda true," Charlie said, surprising JJ. "Yes, getting exposure on social media is definitely possible, but given it's a global network, you'd probably have a huge percentage of followers from places too far away to add any real foot traffic to the store. Plus, the effort of posting and staying active on these platforms each week can get distracting."

JJ tipped his cup back to get the last swallow of smoothie as he considered Charlie's words. "So you're saying social media won't increase our Suspects lever at all?"

"Not exactly," Charlie countered. "What I am saying is that it won't increase your Suspects in the way you've been thinking—and in the way most business owners use it. See, most social media platforms do allow you to increase your Suspects through targeted advertising. You can pay to run specific targeted advertisements to people whose interests, location, and demographics fit your ideal Suspect. This way there is no noise, no wastage reaching people on the other side of the globe, and no need to keep your account up-to-date. So, yes, social media platforms can definitely help you increase your Suspects lever very efficiently when you know why and how to use them properly."

Having covered the back of his training schedule, Charlie fished another piece of paper out of his bag and wrote the following:

> **Suspects**: *Social media might drive more visitors to the store, yes, but they might not be the kind you want to reach.*

> **Prospects**: *It won't really help you increase your Prospects, or the number of people self-selecting.*

Conversions: It doesn't really help you increase sales because sales happen in the store.

Average Item Price: It is unlikely to allow you to increase your prices.

Items per Sale: You can't sell access to your social media, so it's not something to help increase items per sale.

Transactions per Customer: It can increase repeat transactions by reminding customers about product life cycles, new releases, etc.—but the impact would be relatively small.

Margins: It can't really help you negotiate with Jules or any other suppliers.

Charlie turned the paper around to show JJ. "Does this make sense?" he asked.

"Yeah, I think so," JJ said after a short pause. "What you've just done is really interesting. You've kind of turned the concept of the *7 Levers* on its head and used it as a type of filter, a way for me to stop wasting time, stay focused, and be clear on how social media can grow the business."

"A filter—that's a great way of thinking about it," Charlie said. "And the thing is, for another business thinking about using social media and doing the same process, using the *7 Levers* as a filter might get a totally different outcome. For example, a friend of mine has an online skincare label. Given that she ships her products globally, she uses social media a great deal to increase her profits. She uses it to launch new products and keep in touch with their customer base. Plus, they can extend their network by having customers or celebrities showcase their products on their own social media pages. They can use different hashtags to attract attention from people who could be a target for a certain type of product…and so forth. They don't have the same geographical restrictions you have with the store and no one else is selling their brand, so they can use social media to increase different levers because of that."

"I'm getting the feeling it would be the same thing for the podcast," JJ said, a little disheartened.

"Maybe…you tell me," Charlie responded, smiling.

JJ excused himself to use the men's room to give himself time to think. Upon his return, he told Charlie, "Well, I got some ideas. They might be a little crazy, but here goes."

"Fire away," Charlie said.

"First of all, I might be able to convince some of my suppliers to give us some price breaks if we feature and talk about their products or athletes on the podcast—a little cash-for-comment type arrangement," JJ began. "If we sent each new podcast episode out to the database of customers we're now building, this might overcome the problem with getting customers to proactively subscribe to the show…and could be a great excuse for a weekly email. I couldn't think of a way the podcast would allow us to increase our Items per Sale or the Average Item Price, so no *10% Win* there."

Charlie nodded, encouraging him to go on.

"I'm sure we'll be able to build up a reasonable listener base of local athletes who could be potential customers, but again, would you really drive all the way across town to buy a bike? Not many would. Unless we started to record the show live in-store and make a bit of an event out of it. So I think until we get an online store and a way to easily reach a wider audience, a podcast probably isn't a good fit for our business right now."

"Spot on," Charlie said enthusiastically. "It's so easy to get caught up in the hype or all the online chatter about the newest tool or the tactic and feel you have to apply it to your business like everyone else is. Maybe it could be useful for you down the line, but for now, you should be focusing on the lower-hanging fruit—the things that will give you the biggest *10% Wins* with the least amount of effort possible."

"By running any tool, strategy, or tactic through the *7 Levers* as a filter, you can see where it could fit and gauge whether the idea is strong enough to give you a *10% Win*. So when you next cycle through that lever, you've got a clear idea on what to implement."

JJ couldn't help but be impressed with his unintentional business coach. Charlie never ceased to surprise him with his business acumen.

"Take video, for example," Charlie said. "A few weeks ago, you mentioned that Emma from your store suggested creating a bunch of videos to give away to customers as a way to justify a higher price per item—i.e. more value for a higher price."

"That's right. I thought it was a great idea," JJ said.

"If we run 'video' through the filter, where else can you use it to get a *10% Win*?" Charlie asked.

"Well, we can create a bunch of videos to use for the social media advertisements. Not social media posts, but actual ads," JJ said.

"Perfect, so when it comes time to work on your Suspects lever, you can pull the camera out and record some short social media-style commercials and post them online."

"From what I've read and seen, video works really well on e-commerce sites to increase Prospects and Conversions, but that doesn't really fit Cadence," JJ said.

"Spot on," Charlie said, "and what you're already doing with the videos to justify the higher price is brilliant. But what about creating a more detailed video series and selling it as a standalone training course? Something you can use to increase Items per Sale?"

"That's a great idea. Emma's been wanting to create some more detailed videos for a while, but we were not sure of the point," JJ said excitedly. "We've just started sending the email sequence out to clients after the purchase, which seems to be going well, even though it's early. We've been able to stop giving discounts all the time, which has resulted in a 5% increase across the board on all our bikes and a 10% increase on the really high-end ones."

Charlie nodded his encouragement. "Great, although the podcast idea is on ice, you could create a few videos to include in your email sequence actually showing people how to tell when their tires need replacing, or their bike chain needs a service. That will surely increase the repeat purchase rate and give your Transactions per Customer an additional *10% Win*.

"So along with using the *7 Levers* as a *framework* to focus your time and attention toward increasing profits, you can also use it as a *filter* to find the best way to use a tool and tactic for your business—and discover where and how it can give you *10% Wins* in one of the seven key areas of business profits."

Charlie and JJ parted in the parking lot of the aquatic center, planning to meet up again early the following week for one last training session at the track. The following week, Charlie would head to New Zealand for the IRONMAN competition.

As he turned to head for his Jeep, JJ couldn't help but feel as if the intuitive sense he got about Charlie the first time they met had far exceeded his expectations. He hoped Charlie could say the same for him.

Chapter 16

The Finish Line

A few days before Charlie's IRONMAN, JJ was back in the storeroom at Cadence going over the weekly numbers. As he started tallying his sales for his ProSport account, he noticed a knot forming in his stomach and realized he was already preparing for the worst. He realized that the summer was almost over and, if he wanted to get the target rebate that he'd negotiated with Jules, he'd have to see if he reached his sales benchmarks for the season. He held his breath as he did the calculations.

He couldn't believe it. Combining all of the strategies he'd tried so far, his Average Item Price was up 8%. And thanks to the new sales initiative among his team and the cycling checklists they'd started using, Conversions and Items per Sale were up 16% and 18%, respectively. He then tallied the sales for ProSport and felt the tension leave his body for the first time in months.

He put down his pen and reached for the office phone, dialing Jules's number as quickly as his fingers could manage. He was actually shaking a little from excitement.

"Jules, it's JJ. I believe you owe me some money," he said coyly.

"What do you mean?" Jules said, taken off guard.

"I was just looking at my numbers, and it appears I have reached the next ProSport discount level—a few weeks ahead of schedule according to my calendar. I believe that entitles me to a rebate?"

Jules laughed. "That's fabulous, JJ! Congrats. We'll have to verify the numbers on our end, of course, but if all looks in order, we'll get that rebate to you right away. By the way, how's the simulator working out for you?"

"It's been great! Customers love it, and I've definitely increased sales of our higher-quality bikes because of it. I've even managed to sell several simulators since we had it installed."

"I noticed that! We're happy to have you as our customer, JJ."

"Thanks, Jules."

JJ hung up the phone feeling better than he had in ages. He knew he still had a way to go before he would be a millionaire, but sales were definitely increasing the more he worked the *7 Levers* Charlie had taught him. And for the first time in a while, he wasn't worried about money. He felt like celebrating, so he picked up the phone again.

"Sarah, it's me. What do you have going on this weekend?"

* * * * *

"I need a kiss for good luck," Charlie said as he leaned down to take Chloe's face in his hands.

"Muu-ahh," she said as she gave him an exaggerated smack on the lips. "Knock 'em dead, baby. You've earned this."

Charlie could feel the adrenaline pumping through his veins. He'd been warming up for the past hour, and now his body was ready. If they didn't start the competition soon, he felt like he would explode.

As he scanned the crowd of athletes gathered at the shore of the ocean, he spotted a familiar figure against the lush landscape. "JJ?!" Charlie shouted, startling Chloe.

JJ ran over to Charlie, and Charlie noticed Sarah walking behind him holding the hands of two adorable children. "Hey champ!" JJ said, patting his trainee on the back. "Surprise!"

"I had no idea you were coming! This is awesome!"

"Neither did I, actually," JJ said as Sarah and the twins joined him at his side. "Turns out, you were right about the *7 Levers*, and things are going so well at the store I decided to splurge and take the family on a last-minute vacation so we could cheer you on."

"I promise to make you proud, coach," Charlie said as an announcer called for all of the athletes to get ready at the start line. "Gotta go! Meet you at the finish line?"

"Wouldn't miss it!" JJ called. Charlie gave Chloe another quick kiss and sprinted off.

"We're so glad you guys could make it. Want to join me in the cabana for a mimosa over breakfast while Charlie sweats it out? I can't think of a better way to celebrate." She winked at Sarah.

"We'll be there in a minute," Sarah said. "Order us whatever you prefer." Sarah turned her face up toward JJ's. "It's so beautiful here. Thank you so much." She squeezed JJ tight as Ben and Emily also crowded in for a family hug.

As the family walked toward the cabana for breakfast, JJ spotted a familiar face in the crowd. "Dale?" JJ called.

Dale spun around. "Oh my god! Hi JJ!"

"What are you doing here? IRONMAN distances aren't your thing."

"I know. I'm not here to race," Dale said. "I'm glad I ran into you. I've been wanting to tell you that getting fired from Cadence was the best thing that ever happened to me. I've been getting podiums for the past few years as you know, but I took your advice and decided to throw all my focus on going pro."

"Oh yeah?" JJ asked.

"Yep, I'm actually on my way to Boulder, Colorado. There's a huge triathlete community there, and I've already got my first sponsors lined up. In fact, it was a sponsor who brought me here. So you won't be seeing me around the old hometown anymore."

"Good for you," JJ said. "I wish you the best."

"I have you to thank for it, JJ. If you hadn't let me go, I probably wouldn't have taken the chance. You really did me a favor."

JJ was glad to hear this, but he didn't know what else to say. "Well, listen, good luck. I'll be watching out for you on those pro podiums." Dale smiled and turned to head to the edge of the lake.

"Daddy up!" Emily squealed. JJ said goodbye to Dale and picked the twins up, one in each arm.

"Happy Daddy!" Ben yelled, clearly noticing the wide grin on JJ's face.

"Happy Daddy, indeed," JJ said.

* * * * *

"You…are…an…IRONMAN!" JJ congratulated Charlie after he crossed the finish line in under twelve hours, just like he'd hoped. The newly minted IRONMAN was exhausted but beaming from ear to ear.

"Couldn't have done it without you, coach! Thanks for cheering me on for the past twenty weeks."

The following night, JJ and Sarah left the kids with the hotel's childcare and joined Chloe and Charlie for a celebratory dinner at a beautiful restaurant overlooking the beach. Sarah looked ravishing in the dress JJ had bought her for their last anniversary...and the new shoes he'd surprised her with on the way to the airport.

"To Charlie!" JJ said, as he raised his wine glass for a toast. "Not just for his amazing accomplishment yesterday, but for all of the hard work and discipline he spent getting there. Thank you for being one of the best trainees I've ever coached. You were willing to learn and listen, and always eager to do the things you knew you needed to do to improve, even if it wasn't always easy to see the finish line."

"And to JJ," Charlie continued. "For doing the same thing."

The Seven Levers Framework

Whether you run a brick-and-mortar retail business like JJ or work in e-commerce, B2B, wholesale, the service industry, or any other field, you can apply the *7 Levers* framework to help you reach *10% Wins* and double your profits in no time. Just cycle through each of the levers and you'll have a consistent strategy for tremendous long-term growth.

Suspects: The amount of traffic you get to your store or website is extremely important, but it is only one of the levers of growth. Many business owners make the mistake of focusing on increasing Suspects exclusively and generally lack a strategy for doing so efficiently. Use the marketing hierarchy to identify the lowest-hanging fruit—the searchers who are actively interested in purchasing your product or service—and target them before trying to reach less motivated suspects.

Prospects: Not every Suspect with whom you interact will be interested in buying from you, but those who are will always engage in some action that indicates they are ready to be sold to. Define what this action is for your business. It might be built into your business model—like asking for a quote or adding items to a shopping cart—or you might have to get more creative like JJ did by installing a simulator at Cadence. Once you have identified your Prospects, you can change the conversation you have with them to be more direct in helping them find whatever it is they need.

Conversions: Prospects may be motivated, but they don't actually put money in your pocket until they buy from you. In order to convert Prospects to sales, be active, not passive, in engaging with them. People favor businesses that they can trust and that provide good customer service by helping them find exactly what they need—even if they aren't quite sure what it is themselves.

Items per Sale: Obviously, the more items someone buys from you, the more revenue you'll make. Sometimes a customer may not be aware that they are on the market for something until they know it exists. What additional products or services can you offer that would appeal to your target customer? How can you organize your store or website design so that customers are alerted to other things they might need? What can you offer to them that you're currently not offering?

Average Item Price: While certain business owners can simply increase the price of their product or service based on demand, if customers cannot distinguish between your offering and that of your competitors', this is not an option for you. Instead, you need to practice the art of perceived value by giving something extra to the customer that will justify the increase in cost. Is it a complimentary service? A guarantee or warranty? A better experience? Don't hesitate to look for examples of this from other industries.

Transactions per Customer: Once you've made the sale, how do you get the customer to return to your business? If you already have loyal customers but your business doesn't provide services or products that people need regularly—as was the case with Charlie's accountant Don—think of new ways you can get them to come back. It's also important to stay in touch with customers—whether through email, social media, events, or whatever works for your particular business—so you are top of mind when the time comes for them to buy again.

Margins: The above six levers will all help increase revenue, but in order to increase profits, you need to keep margins as low as possible. Where can you cut costs associated with running your business? Take a quick audit of all of your expenses and eliminate what you don't need. Don't hesitate to call up suppliers to see if they offer packages that may be less expensive for your business needs.

* * * * *

Don't be a stranger, we'd love to hear about all your 10% Wins!

Come join the 10% Win Club at www.cadencebook.com/extra

If you'd like more information on how to implement the 7 Levers in your business, you're invited to join a program that will walk you through the *Clarify & Capture, Calculate & Correct,* and *Create & Cycle* process at
www.cadencebook.com/extra

And read more from Pete at
www.PreneurMarketing.com

About the Author

Pete Williams is an entrepreneur, advisor and marketer who Forbes recently called, *"one entrepreneur today that every marketer should be modeling,"* while Inc. describes him as, *"a savvy marketing strategist."*

A Southern Region Finalist in the Ernst & Young Entrepreneur of the Year Program, a Small Business ICON (Best-in-Class) Recipient, and an Australian Business Award Winner for Marketing Excellence, he is the co-founder of numerous businesses across varying industries—from telecommunications services to e-commerce.

Having been referred to as "Australia's Richard Branson" in media publications, Pete first made a name for himself when, at age twenty-one, he sold Australia's version of Yankee Stadium, the Melbourne Cricket Ground, for under $500—which you can read about in his first book, *How to Turn Your Million-Dollar Idea Into a Reality* (2007).

Pete's companies include Infiniti Telecommunications, SimplyHeadsets.com.au, SpringCom Telecommunications, and Preneur Group (www.PreneurMarketing.com), an advisory-consulting firm that guides business owners through the process of increasing profits, margins and other key indicators by using the *7 Levers* approach to business growth.

Pete is also a Professor-of-Practice at Deakin University, Australia, where he works with marketing and business students to give them real-world experience as part of their education.

Pete splits his time between Melbourne, Australia and California, USA with his wife Fleur and son Eli.

He completed his first IRONMAN triathlon in under 12 hours after just 20 weeks of training from his coach James.

Acknowledgements

To Dom Goucher, thanks for being there from the start, mate. The *7 Levers* framework wouldn't have grown into what it is today if it wasn't for the input, support and effort you put in to make it all happen. Your DNA is embedded throughout everyone's *10% Wins*.

To Angie Kiesling, thanks for helping form my jumbled thoughts into coherent words. From the moment this booked changed from a traditional non-fiction book to the story it became, you helped craft the characters and create a compelling narrative—something I could have never done on my own.

To Brooke Carey, thanks for taking that original story and editing it into something far better than I thought it could ever be. Your editing, experience and guidance from working on another fabulous business parable was truly invaluable and made this book something I am so very proud of.

To John Warrillow and Neil Strauss, thanks for both independently leading me to Brooke.

To graphic designer Nathan Fisher (a *Preneur Advisory Board* member), thanks for creating all the amazing notebook sketches in the book.

To Margo, Bethany, Jim, David, and their entire Morgan James Team, thanks for making my decision to turn down traditional publishing offers and release this book with you—the right one. Your patience, support and guidance made it a really fun and rewarding experience.

To Troy, Adam and all my business partners (across the journey), thanks for letting our projects be the test tube for a lot of the lessons learnt and shared in this book.

To my wife Fleur and son Eli, thanks for putting up with me, my schedule and my habits. I often joke that you knew what you were getting into when you started dating me all those years ago, and that Eli has just grown up with it. But if it wasn't for all the love, support and flexibility you give me, I wouldn't be able to do what I enjoy each and every day.

To all the customers of our projects, advisory board members, consulting clients, and the followers of all my work—thank you! Your trust and support means the world to me.

And as I said at the start of this book with the dedication—to all the entrepreneurs, small-business owners, managers and marketers, I acknowledge all those sleepless nights, stressful mornings, risks and rewards. It's because of you that the economy grows and the world turns!

A Final Word

The open road of business ownership can be a very lonely place.

You can't bitch about the boss with your co-worker. You can't depend on anyone else to bail you out in an emergency. You can't enjoy the normal hours and regular vacations that come with a typical job. Ultimately, you are the only person responsible for whether the business lives or dies.

Every business and every entrepreneur needs support, direction and encouragement occasionally. I hope this book has been a little of each for you.

If it has, perhaps there's someone else in your network who you could now help.

If you've taken anything from this book, highlighted a paragraph, made a note in the margins, or just giggled at one of Charlie's bad puns, I hope you'll pay it forward and share this book with a fellow entrepreneur.

As you know, it's a short yet powerful story that could quickly change their business trajectory.

Suggest they read it on their next flight, or listen during their commute to the office.

Help them to get rolling with their own set of *10% Wins*.

Contrary to outside perception, both triathlon and business really are team sports!

Morgan James
Speakers Group

www.TheMorganJamesSpeakersGroup.com

We connect Morgan James published authors with live and online events and audiences who will benefit from their expertise.

Morgan James makes all of our titles available
through the Library for All Charity Organization.

www.LibraryForAll.org

CPSIA information can be obtained
at www.ICGtesting.com
Printed in the USA
BVHW07s2022121018

53009TBV00003B/5/P